Portraits of
the Savior

PORTRAITS OF THE SAVIOR

BY DR. HERBERT LOCKYER

*"Have I been so long time with you, and yet
hast thou not known me?" (John 14:9)*

Thomas Nelson Publishers
Nashville • Camden • New York

Copyright © 1983 by Herbert Lockyer

Published in Nashville, Tennessee, by Thomas Nelson, Inc. and distributed in Canada by Lawson Falle, Ltd., Cambridge, Ontario.

Printed in the United States of America.

Library of Congress Cataloging in Publication Data

Lockyer, Herbert.
    Portraits of the Savior.

    1. Jesus Christ—Person and offices.   I. Title.
BT202.L582 1983   232   83-2324
ISBN 0-8407-5288-1
ISBN 0-8407-5838-3 (pbk.)

CONTENTS

PREFACE

Have you met Jesus?

Most of us sing, talk, and argue about Him. We try to feel His nearness. But He is not real to us. The tragedy is that Christ is not, to us, the living, bright Reality He ought to be.

He once lived here on this planet. Devout souls, gazing into His noble, heavenly face, found it easy to love Him. Our difficulty, however, is that we have never seen Jesus. Our vision of Him is one of faltering faith. We find it difficult to love One whose presence is unclear.

I have written this book because I want Jesus to be clear and near to you. Yet, my task is an impossible one. I agree with the modest words of Dr. Alexander Stewart, one-time professor of systematic theology in St. Andrew's University, Scotland, who in 1906 wrote his *Life of Christ*. He said, "He who would worthily write the life of Jesus Christ must have a pen dipped in the imaginative sympathy of a poet, in the prophet's fire, in the artist's charm and grace, and in the reverence and purity of a saint."

I don't claim to have painted the portraits in this book. They have been painted by the Holy Spirit. Christ's parting gift to His own was the encouraging Holy Spirit who came to make Jesus real to believing hearts. The Spirit reveals Christ in all His fullness to us. Through the portraits He paints, the Holy Spirit begets love for the Savior.

May the selfsame Spirit be pleased to use the meditations of this book for the deepening of your affection for Him.

I want to request that you approach these pages with the attitude of the Greeks who said to the apostle Philip: "Sir, we would see Jesus" (John 12:21).

1

A Perfect Self-Portrait

Jesus Himself should have the first place in this study. I invite you to examine what Jesus said about Himself before we move on to discover what others said about Him. Only as we know all that He was can we judge His fitness to be the complete revelation of God. We will not stop with this knowledge. We will go on to act on it.

True Christian experience is essentially a relationship with Christ. Such a relationship is crucial. If we are honest in our belief that Jesus is God's revelation of Himself to mankind, then we shall submit ourselves to His instructions. We will fashion our lives according to His teaching. We will become His faithful disciples. Are you ready for this deepened relationship?

Jesus is the one character in human history of whom more has been written and spoken than any other person. Where is the library large enough to contain all the books, booklets, and tracts produced through the last nineteen hundred years, dealing with the pre-existence, incarnation, life, character, virtues, teachings, miracles, death, resurrection, ascension, and the present and future ministry of Jesus? How many millions of sermons have been preached on His uniqueness, grace, and power? Who could number the host of pastors and Christian workers who, every Sunday, wherever they witness on the face of the earth, magnify and extol Him as Savior and Lord?

Friends and foes alike have uttered widely differing opinions about Jesus, who never ceases to be the center of universal attraction. When He lived among men, there was a division because of Him. Some held that He was a deceiver, impostor, winebibber, madman—possessed of a devil; others declared Him a great prophet of righteousness, a good man, the wisest of teachers, a beautiful character, and God manifest in flesh. But although it is interesting and profitable to gather together all that men have said about Jesus, the opinion of Him that matters most is the one He held concerning Himself. We can have no higher authority of who He is than what He taught regarding Himself.

Jesus had no doubt whatever as to who He was, from where He came, why He entered our world, and what the future held for Him. Authoritatively and unequivocally, He affirmed His claims even though they aroused fierce antagonisms and resulted, from the human standpoint, in His crucifixion. What were these affirmations and claims of One who could not lie?

HIS PRE-EXISTENCE

Although it may sound somewhat paradoxical, this statement is perfectly true: *Jesus lived before He was born!* His beginning as the *Word* was long before His beginning as *man* (see John 1:1). In fact, He existed before all time. There never was a time when He was not. In the prologue to the fourth Gospel, John, in three crisp sentences, announces the way in which Jesus antedated the beginning of all things: (1) His Eternal existence—"In the beginning was the Word"; (2) His Eternal intercommunion with the Father—"the Word was with God"; (3) His Eternal identity with the Godhead—"the Word was God" (John 1:1).

Jesus came as "The everlasting Father" (Is. 9:6) and as the "lofty One that inhabiteth eternity" (Is. 57:15). His advent on earth out of a past eternity is implied in His claim, "Before Abraham was, I am" (John 8:58). Quite openly, Jesus spoke of the glory He had with God the Father before the creation of the world and also of His coming forth from the Father (see John 16:28). In His conversation with Nicodemus, Jesus asserted that He came down from heaven (see John 3:13). He came, then, as the eternal Son of God.

John had no hesitation in declaring that Jesus not only antedated all things but was Creator of them: "All things were made by him; and without him was not any thing made that was made" (John 1:3). Thus, Jesus was taken out of the category of created beings altogether. Accordingly, what is said of Him is not that He was the first of existences to come into being—"in the beginning he already had come into being"—but that in the beginning, when things began to come into being, He already was. Here is found Christ's pre-existence. By his probing language, John would have us realize that Jesus as the Word was the eternal Son of the Father who shared fully the divine nature. This was the Word that became flesh, who, while assuming our full humanity, did so without in any way diminishing His Deity.

HIS MESSIAHSHIP

The Old Testament presents us with the heaven-drawn picture of the Messiah who was to come.

In the Gospels, the expected One steps down out of

the frame in the person of Christ, a name also meaning "the anointed one." When Andrew, after his surrender to Jesus, went out to find his brother, Simon Peter, to tell him the good news, he exclaimed, "We have found the Messias, which is, being interpreted, the Christ" (John 1:41).

More explicit is the expression of the Samaritan woman who, during a spiritual conversation with the Stranger she met at the well, confessed her faith in the long-promised Messiah: "I know that Messias cometh, which is called Christ: when he is come, he will tell us all things" (John 4:25).

Without hesitation, Jesus immediately replied, "I that speak unto thee am *he* [the Messiah]" (John 4:26). Leaving her waterpot at the well, the woman hurried back and confessed to her fellow Samaritans, "Come, see a man, which *told me all things that ever I did:* [the woman's own description of the authoritative Messiah] is not this *the* Christ?" (John 4:29, italics added).

When Jesus urged His disciples to search the Old Testament books, saying "they . . . testify of me" (John 5:39), He actually identified Himself with Daniel's prophecy of "Messiah the Prince" (Dan. 9:25) who would come and vindicate his claim as God's Anointed One. Further, when Jesus spoke of Himself as "the Son of David" and as "the Son of man," He used prophetic messianic titles. Jesus constantly related Himself to the past and identified Himself as the promised Messiah of Israel.

The prewritten life of Jesus has been an astounding miracle to me as I have compared it with the perfect fulfillment in the Jesus of history. I agree with Dr. A. T. Pierson who says in *Knowing the Scriptures:*

> The inspiration of that portrait came from the Heavenly Gallery, and not from the studio of an artist. . . . Noth-

ing but Divine prescience could have foreseen it, and nothing but Divine power could accomplish it.

In Jesus' simple, poor home at Nazareth, a religious atmosphere prevailed. In the synagogue, Jesus listened to the Old Testament, any scroll of which was deemed precious. While as God the Son, His mission was eternally clear, nonetheless in His young humanity, the more He listened, the deeper the conviction grew that He was the promised *Christ*. The Greek equivalent for *Messiah*, is correctly rendered in English by the word *anointed*. Striking, is it not, that when He entered His public ministry, one day He rebuked *demons* who, knowing that He was the promised Messiah, confessed, "Thou art Christ" (Luke 4:41)? He did not want such a testimony from them.

HIS HUMANITY

Since I am confining myself to what Jesus Himself actually said about the themes we are considering, it is not my purpose here to elaborate upon the evidences of His humanity which the New Testament states. What I want to stress is His own assumption of humanity that emerges in some of the titles He used of Himself. Two of the titles frequently used are *the Son of man* and *the Son of God*, the main distinction between the two being His relationship to man on earth and His relationship to His Father in heaven.

As *Son of man*, He dwelt here below for over thirty-three years and will return to have dominion over the earth. This title, then, associates Jesus as the One who entered into His own creation, the world, in which the experiences that belong to human beings would also be His. Further, as "the Son of man" He became the prototype of humanity in its most perfect form. The Gospels portray Jesus as the Ideal Man.

Canon Liddon expressed his observations of Christ's human nature, implied by the designation *Son of man*, in this fitting way:

> It does not merely assert his real incorporation with our kind: it exalts him indefinitely above us all as the true representative, the ideal, the pattern Man. His is a Human Life which does justice to the idea of Humanity. He is the Archetypal Man.

The name by which Jesus most frequently designated Himself was *the Son of man*, which occurs some eighty-four times in the Gospels, where the title was *never* used of the Lord by anyone but Himself. In the New Testament, it is only used four times outside the Gospels (see Acts 7:56; Heb. 2:6; Rev. 1:13; 14:14).

However, this was not a title Jesus invented, seeing it occurs in the Old Testament (see Ps. 8:4; 80:17). In Ezekiel it is used no fewer than ninety times. Daniel also employs the title (see Dan. 7:13; 8:17). Jesus never defined the title nor mentioned where He found it or how He came to designate Himself in such a way. As it was His favorite self-designation, He must have felt it was a most appropriate expression for the human side of His person.

Jesus named Himself thus, because, through His incarnation when He became flesh, He belongs to mankind—as one who in human nature has accomplished great things for human beings. He is man, in the supreme sense, who makes real the ideal humanity. He took upon Himself all the attributes belonging to human nature and shared in all that is human, sin excepted.

Allied to the title *Son of man* is another expressing His humanity, namely, *Jesus,* recurring about 240 times in the Gospels. This personal birthname of His is the Greek form of a Hebrew name found in *Joshua*, the successor to Moses, and in *Jeshua*, the high priest. Its full form is *Jehoshua*, (see Num. 13:16) meaning, "Jehovah our salvation." It is used by and for Jesus in association with the saving work He was to accomplish as the *Man* Christ Jesus. The most striking use of such a precious name was when Jesus appeared to Saul of Tarsus on his way to persecute Christ's followers (see Acts 9:5).

How sweet the name of Jesus sounds in a believer's ear!
It soothes his sorrows, heals his wounds,
And drives away his fear.

Evident proofs of His humanity are not difficult to trace in the Gospel narratives:

He identified Himself with men (see Matt. 4:4; Luke 4:4).

He behaved in human ways (see Matt. 11:19; Luke 7:34).

He made frequent references to His body and its parts (see Matt. 26:12,26; Mark 14:8,22; Luke 7:44–46; 22:19–20; 24:39).

He referred to human dread as he confronted death (see Luke 22:42).

He gave expression to his sense of desolation on the cross (see Matt. 27:46; Mark 15:34).

He understood evil, without participating in it (see Matt. 7:11; 9:12; 12:34,39; Luke 11:13,29).

O Saviour Christ, Thou too art Man;
Thou has been troubled, tempted, tried;
Thy kind but searching glance can scan
The very wounds that shame would hide.

HIS DEITY

Dr. Benjamin B. Warfield, in his monumental work *The Lord of Glory,* states emphatically, "Those who will not have a divine Christ must seek their human Jesus outside the entire evangelical literature." Thus, we who are biblical Christians affirm without hesitation that "the Son of man" and "the Son of God" are one and the same person. Jesus was God manifest in flesh and, coming as the one who in a past eternity was *equal with God,* manifested divine attributes while among men. In the Stranger of Galilee, Deity and humanity were happily wed. The Holy Spirit tied a love knot between His two natures in the womb of Mary. Thus Jesus came as Mary's first-born Son and as God's beloved Son.

It is perfectly clear from our Lord's own teachings that He claimed to have a filial relationship with the Father, had unity and equality with God, coupling His own name with that of the Father in a most natural way. Categorically, Jesus declared Himself to be "the Son of God," thereby "making himself equal with God" (John 5:18). God Himself, the angel Gabriel, the disciples, and even evil spirits alike spoke of Jesus as "the Son of God." And the expressions of His Deity, which He repeatedly used, are most impressive. The title *Son of God* is found also thirty times in the Gospels and elsewhere in the New Testament some twenty times.

He unhesitatingly allowed Himself to be called *God* (see John 10:33; 20:28).

His various "I am's" can be claimed only for Deity (see John 14:6).

His assertion of being the sole Mediator between God and man likewise affirms His Deity (see John 10:9). In the fourth Gospel, He did not hesitate to proclaim His Godhead (see John 10:30; 14:9).

He manifested, as well as confessed, the possession of divine attributes. *Omnipotence*, for instance, is asserted in His commission to His disciples: "*All* power is given unto me in heaven and in earth" (Matt. 28:18). His many miracles prove His sovereignty in every realm (see Mark 2:1–12). He has all power.

Jesus, likewise, claimed the further divine attribute of *omniscience*. Knowing what was in man, He surprised Nathanael when He told him, "When thou wast under the fig tree, I saw thee" (John 1:48). "He knew what was in man" (John 2:25). The Gospels give us other instances of His perfect knowledge. He knows all things.

He also manifested the attribute of *omnipresence*, the ability to be everywhere at the same time. He assured His disciples that wherever they gathered in His name, He would be there in the midst of them and that He would never leave nor forsake them (see Matt. 28:20; Heb. 13:5). He is present with us today.

When Jesus made use on His own initiative of the abbreviated form *the Son*, it was evidently with the same force as the self-designation of "the Son of God." It is true that this term is applied to angels, to men, to the Jewish nation as a whole, to Jewish kings, and to all saints, but as Dr. Stalker observes in his *Ethic of Jesus*, "The principal ideas which the term embodies are, that those bearing the name are derived from God as their Author, that they are the objects of His love and choice, and that they are like Him in character and conduct." With Jesus as "the Son of God," these ideas reach perfection. When He used the expression, it indicated His relationship to God was not only unique, but "one that reached up beyond the competency of men or angels, till He named Himself in the same breath with the Father and the Holy Spirit as an object of worship."

The Jews knew the miracles of Jesus were not merely

signs of unusual power but also disturbing proofs of His divine commission. They understood them, along with His words, as the substantiation of His claim to be equal with God (see John 5:1–19; 10:30–33; 14:8–11). The purpose of John both in his Gospel and in his three Epistles was to show that Jesus is "the true God" who was "made flesh" (John 1:14). John's designations of Him as "God" and as "the Son of God" declare an entirely unique and eternal relationship, which Jesus Himself declared constitutes the only ground of His appeal to men to come to Him to learn of God (see Matt. 11:27). As Dr. Warfield puts it:

> Speaking in the most solemn manner, He not only presents himself as the Son, as the sole source of knowledge of God, and of blessedness for men, but places Himself in a position, not of equality merely, but of absolute reciprocity and interpenetration of knowledge of the Father, as if the being of the Son were so immense that only God would know it thoroughly, and the knowledge of the Son so unlimited that He could know God to perfection.

The evidence of the Deity of Jesus, then, is the warp and woof of the Gospels. A threefold cord that cannot be broken proves his position in the Godhead:

• His assertions of equality with God the Father (see John 5:17–18; 10:30).
• His prerogative to forgive sins (see Matt. 9:6; Mark 2:7,10).
• His authority to give eternal life to all who believe (see John 10:28).

This marvelous truth of God in Christ solves all our problems and makes all things possible. In "A Death in the Desert," Browning imagines the death and last words of the apostle:

> I say, the acknowledgement of God in Christ
> Accepted by thy reason, solves for thee
> All questions in the earth and out of it.

How blessed we are if out of a redeemed, adoring heart we can exclaim with Thomas as we gaze at the crucified, risen Savior—*"My Lord and my God!"* (John 20:28).

HIS PERFECTION

Jesus is the only perfect person the world has ever known. Apart from Him, *"all* have sinned" (Rom. 3:23, italics added). For any person to say, "I have never sinned," would not only be false but presumptuous. Yet the Man of Galilee could stand before men and ask, "Which of you convinceth [convicts] me of sin?" (John 8:46). In every other individual, original sin can be found, and the old Adamic nature gives Satan a foothold. But Jesus could say, "The prince of this world cometh, and hath nothing in me" (John 14:30). There was nothing within Him to which Satan could appeal or use.

The sinlessness and Deity of Jesus are implied in the announcement of Gabriel to Mary, "that *holy thing* which shall be born of thee shall be called the Son of God" (Luke 1:35, italics added). Had Jesus sinned, even once, He would have forfeited His right to die as a ransom for sin. It is His perfection that gives efficacy to His death for sinners.

> He only could unlock the gate of Heaven,
> And let us in.

When the scribes and Pharisees brought a woman, taken in the very act of adultery, to Jesus, they tried to trap Him by saying, "Moses in the law commanded us, that such should be stoned: but what sayest thou?" (John 8:5).

Jesus, as though He had not heard them, stooped and wrote something with His finger in the dust—the only reference to His writing. Then looking up, He said to His foes, "He that is without sin among you, [could He have meant the particular sin of which men had made the woman guilty?] let him first cast a stone at her" (John 8:7). Then He continued writing.

When the woman's accusers heard the answer of Jesus, they, conscience-stricken, left him "one by one, beginning at the eldest" (John 8:9). The only man present who was without sin was Jesus, but He never cast a stone. Graciously He said, "Neither do I condemn thee: go, and sin no more" (John 8:11). Because He was the sinless one, He had the authority and was willing to forgive, for "who can forgive sins but God only?" (Mark 2:7).

The psalmist urges us, "Mark the perfect man, and behold the upright: for the end of that man is peace" (Ps. 37:37). Only in the Man Christ Jesus can there be found this combination of perfection and peace. Not only was He undefiled, but He was also undefilable. His untainted holiness was such that, although tempted by Satan, He never yielded. No temptation could fasten itself upon Him. Although in close contact with sin, as the Friend of sinners, He remained pure and holy, just as a sunbeam is uncontaminated although it constantly shines on a heap of rubbish. Jesus will ever remain God's perfect Man and man's perfect God.

HIS UNIQUENESS

Any reader of the four Gospels is profoundly impressed with the way Jesus asserted for Himself a peculiar dignity, and for His work, a peculiar efficacy. He comes before us as One having a unique, eternal relationship with the Father, as One who is in the world to accomplish a unique task. Jesus, likewise, has the authority to make unique demands or claims upon us. He calls Himself not *a* Son but *the* Son (see Matt. 11:27). Because of His unique relationship to the Father, He has the right to make upon the other children of God a demand for faith and obedience. If we seek the reasons for claims without parallel in any other person, we can find them in three particulars:

• Jesus is in the Father's confidence, and from Him the other children obtain their knowledge of the Father (see Luke 10:22).

• Jesus fully possessed the privileges and fulfilled the obligations involved in sonship (see John 8:29).

• Jesus, by His death, procured for His own the highest blessings (see Mark 14:24).

The absolutely filial Jesus, then, perfectly fulfilling His Father's will, earned the right to exercise all authority. In virtue of His death and resurrection, He could declare, "All power is given unto me" (Matt. 28:18). As for His unique claims, people who try to deny them always fail.

He claimed absolute authority and infallibility as a teacher. He declared that only He knew the mind of God the Father and that only He could reveal him (see Luke 10:16; John 5:24).

He affirmed that heaven and earth would pass away, but that His authoritative words would never pass away (see Matt. 24:35).

He declared that He came not only to teach the truth, but was the personification of the truth (see John 14:6).

He proclaimed the august power of judging men and allotting them to their eternal destiny, asserting that the

Father had committed all judgment to Him (see John 5:22).

He united Himself with the Father and the Spirit as together constituting the Godhead (see Matt. 28:19).

He not only predicted the fact and manner of His death, but He also claimed the power to lay down His life and take it up again (see Matt. 16:21; Luke 9:22; 18:31–33; John 10:18).

He also claimed that His death was not inevitable but voluntary (see John 10:17). He pointed out that His death had a universal significance (see John 12:32–33), that it had a bearing upon the unseen world (see John 12:31), that it was the purpose of His incarnation (see John 12:27), that it was to be a vicarious death (see Matt. 26:28; Mark 10:45), and that it would eternally glorify the Father (see John 12:28; 13:31; 17:1).

HIS DEATH AND RESURRECTION

Death is an appointment every person must keep. "It is appointed unto men once to die" (Heb. 9:27). At the birth of a baby we never think of it as being born to die but born to *live*. But with Jesus, who came to give His life as a ransom for sinners, it was different. He is the only One in all of history who came into the world for the *purpose* of dying. In a mystery, He died in a past eternity, for He came as the Lamb slain *before* the foundation of the world (see Rev. 13:8). It could almost be said that Jesus was born crucified. Among His many utterances, none is so positive or strikes a grander and more universal note than the one His disciples heard: "The bread that I will give is my flesh, which I will give for the life of the world" (John 6·51)

Jesus Himself declared that His life was not *taken* by others but *given*. "I lay down my life for the sheep. . . . I lay it down of myself. I have power to lay it down, and I have power to take it again" (John 10:15,18).

Such wonderful declarations point back to the sacrificial work of Jesus as conceived and accomplished in the eternal counsel of God. There His self-sacrifice was not *exacted* from Him but was His own spontaneous offering in harmony with His Father's will. At Jesus' trial before Pilate, the ruler was perplexed at the silence of the majestic Prisoner before him and said, "Speakest thou not unto me? knowest thou not that I have power to crucify thee, and have power to release thee?" (John 19:10).

Jesus, breaking His silence, replied, "Thou couldest have no power at all against me, except it were given thee from above" (John 19:11). Here is yet one more proof that His death was voluntary.

That such a death was also vicarious and substitutional comes out in some of Jesus' sayings, "This is my body, which is broken for *you*" (1 Cor. 11:24, italics added). "This is my blood . . . shed for many for the remission of sins" (Matt. 26:28). "The Son of man came . . . to give his life a ransom for many" (Matt. 20:28).

George Bernard Shaw spoke scornfully of those "who actually make their religion centre in the infamy of loading the guilt and punishment of all their sins on an innocent victim." Yet this was what the innocent victim Himself said He would do, namely, die in our stead.

Is it any wonder then that the four Gospels give such space to His death? I want to remind you that two of the Gospels do not tell about the birth of Jesus or relate His Sermon on the Mount in full—Mark and John; but all four narratives record with fullness of detail the fact of His death and resurrection. One third of Matthew, one third of Mark, one fourth of Luke, and one half of John are devoted to the last hours of Jesus.

The prominence given to the death and resurrection of Jesus in the biographies of the Gospels is in strange contrast to the biographies of the notable men in history. For instance, in a biography of Daniel Webster, the American statesman, just five of the 863 pages that deal with his career tell of his death in 1852. Several years ago, a life of the poet Shelley appeared in which just three pages out of a total of 1,389 pages described the sad story of his death by drowning near Leghorn in 1822. In contrast, one third of the Gospels deal with Jesus' death and resurrection.

In the three years of His public ministry, Jesus constantly predicted not only His death but also its manner and purpose. Further, the intensity of the way He felt about the end for which He was born can be seen in the way in which, from the beginning of His ministry, He steadfastly set His face toward Jerusalem where He was to be crucified.

It would take several pages to tabulate all His sayings about His decease at Jerusalem. Here are a few:

"Destroy this temple, and in three days I will raise it up. . . . he spake of the temple of his body" (John 2:19, 21).

"So shall the Son of man be three days and three nights in the heart of the earth" (Matt. 12:40).

"So must the Son of man be lifted up" (John 3:14).

"The Son of man shall be betrayed into the hands of men: And they shall kill him, and the third day he shall be raised again" (Matt. 17:22–23).

In the parable of the vineyard, Jesus portrayed Himself as the Heir the husbandmen would slay (see Matt. 21:33–39). A striking feature of our Lord's frequent references to His death is the way He spoke of it as the great hour of His life and work. It is recorded that His enemies were unable to arrest Him for "*his hour* was not yet come" (John 8:20, italics added). He knew when the hour of His departure would come (John 13:1; 17:1).

When His hour came, He died not as a victim but as a victor, crying with a loud voice, *"It is finished"* (John 19:30). Jesus was not referring to the termination of the terrible anguish He had endured, but to the accomplishment of the task He came from heaven to fulfill. It was thus in anticipation He could pray, "I have finished the work which thou gavest me to do" (John 17:4). This is why many of the old doctrinal preachers referred to the death and resurrection as "the finished work of Christ."

At dark Calvary, He laid hold of the principalities and powers of hell and robbed them forever of their authority. Describing the manner of His death, He said, "I, if I be lifted up . . . will draw all men unto me" (John 12:32). The wondrous cross on which He died as the Prince of glory has never lost its magnetism—and never will—for in heaven the unending song will be, "Worthy is the Lamb that was slain" (Rev. 5:12).

> In the Cross of Christ I glory,
> Towering o'er the wrecks of time;
> All the light of sacred story
> Gathers round its head sublime.

Thus, as James Denny expresses it in *The Death of Christ*, "The forfeiting of His free life has freed our forfeited lives."

With all the foregoing unique claims of Jesus before me, I must agree with the observation of Canon Liddon that "Jesus distinctly, repeatedly, energetically preaches Himself." In any other person the constant *I* would be obnoxious evidence of arrogant presumption. Jesus, however, was all He claimed to be.

You will find only two possible reactions to all His claims and demands, namely, acceptance or rejection.

You must believe Him to be the unique Son of God as He affirmed Himself to be or regard Him as a deceiver and a blasphemer. To all who love and trust Him, He is "the way, the truth, and the life" (John 14:6).

At the conclusion of this chapter on what Jesus claimed about Himself, I feel overwhelmed. The subject is too vast for my mind. I wish I had the ability to expound fully the character, the experience, the excellency, and the greatness of Jesus who had the stamp of perfection imprinted indelibly on all that He did and said! He always did the right thing and uttered the right word. Never once was it necessary for Him to retrace a step or recall a saying. His words were rightly spoken like "apples of gold in pictures of silver" (Prov. 25:11).

His death was loving and courageous. His resurrection was powerful and victorious. Put all of this together—His words, His deeds, His death, His resurrection, and His coming again—and you see the wisdom of Paul's words, "we shall be saved by his life" (Rom. 5:10).

2

His Portrait by Other Biblical Artists

Once you have examined what Jesus claimed about Himself, you can move on to see what others said about Him. Although the marvelous self-portrait of our Savior seems sufficient for our needs, the Holy Spirit saw fit to give us the additional blessing of a portrait painted by other inspired writers of the Bible. This masterpiece is the work of divinely led artists.

I like to compare the colors in this work to those of a rainbow. The several hues of a rainbow seem separate; yet they combine to form a beautiful whole. Likewise, the aspects of Christ's being—His omnipotence, His omniscience, His omnipresence, His eternity, His love, and His humanity—are fused into one marvelous whole in His adorable Person. As it is the province of the Holy Spirit to reveal the facts about Christ to us, let us consider under His inspiration and guidance, all that was involved in the Eternal Son's being made in the likeness of human flesh in order that He might become the

Savior of the world—a central truth around which the whole of Scripture revolves.

CHRIST IN THE OLD TESTAMENT

I wonder if you realize that the first reference in Scripture to Christ is related to His humanity. In the foundational Book of Genesis, you find the cornerstone prediction that He would appear in human form, as He did in "her seed" (Gen. 3:15). This prophecy was fulfilled when Christ was born as Mary's first child (see Matt. 1:16; Luke 2:7–20). It must be noted that He was to come, not from the seed of a woman and a man, through natural conception and birth, but only from the seed of a woman—and a virgin at that (see Is. 7:14). The illustrious Babe of Bethlehem was conceived of the Holy Spirit and born of the Virgin Mary (see Matt. 1:20–23). Although Christ came as the Son of man, He was not the Son of *a* man. He had a human mother but not an earthly father.

The first prediction of His birth also carried the first promise of redemption, for the mission He would accomplish as the seed of the woman, would be the bruising of the serpent's head—accomplished at Calvary when, by His death, He destroyed the power and authority of "that old serpent, called the Devil" (Rev. 12:9). Jesus came "that he might destroy the works of the devil" (1 John 3:8). Since the Cross, Satan has been a defeated foe, and if we resist him with Christ's power, he will flee from us (see James 4:7).

To trace every specific and symbolic reference to Christ in all thirty-nine books of the Old Testament and set them forth would require a large volume of its own. In this chapter, all I can do is to indicate a few of the links in the chain of His humanity as found in some of the Prophets. He, who was before Abraham in the eternal past, could say as He appeared among men, "Abraham rejoiced to see my day: and he saw it, and was glad" (John 8:56). This friend of God was one of those who received from afar the promises of the coming Christ but died in faith before their fulfillment (see Heb. 11:13). It was Abraham who realized that through his own seed "shall all the kindreds of the earth be blessed" (Acts 3:25).

While one could profitably linger over the many prophecies of Christ in Genesis and the following three books of Moses, let us take a leap to Deuteronomy and discover how He would minister when He would enter the body prepared for Him. From Moses came the declaration that Jesus would appear in the nature and likeness of a Jew, as God's Prophet, proclaiming a God-given message—

> The LORD thy God will raise up unto thee a Prophet from the midst of thee, of thy brethren, like unto me; unto him ye shall hearken. . . . I will raise them up a Prophet from among their brethren, like unto thee, and I will put my words in his mouth; and he shall speak unto them all that I shall command him (Deut. 18:15,18).

Peter, in his sermon to Israel, identified Jesus as the Messiah predicted by Moses (see Acts 3:22–23).

Job was another Old Testament saint to whom was given a preview of Him who would come in the likeness of human flesh. In his dramatic book, referred to as "The Matterhorn of the Old Testament," Job affirmed, "I know that my Redeemer liveth, and that he shall stand at the latter day upon the earth" (Job 19:25). Job also had the hope that he would see his Redeemer. "Whom I shall see for myself, and mine eyes shall behold, and not another" (Job 19:27).

Reaching the Psalms, we find them replete with striking foregleams of Christ's first coming to earth, as well as His Second Coming to the world as its rightful Lord and King in order to claim as His inheritance, the uttermost parts of the earth.

We see Jesus as the perfect Man in Psalm 1. No other can answer to the description given of such as He who delights in the law of the Lord (see v. 2).

In Psalm 2, Jesus is depicted as the King that God would set on His holy hill of Zion (see v. 6) and as the One claiming man's affection—"Kiss the Son" (v. 12).

We see Jesus, whose soul and body would be preserved by His Father. "Thou wilt not leave my soul in hell; neither wilt thou suffer thine Holy One to see corruption" (Ps. 16:10). Peter takes this verse and relates it to the resurrection of Christ from the dead (see Acts 2:31). By *hell* or *hades* or *sheol,* the psalmist referred to the sphere of departed spirits which, up until the ascension of Christ, was in two sections, namely *paradise,* the temporary abode of the God-fearing and faithful, and *hell* (the bottomless pit).

Along with the thief, Jesus, at His death, went to paradise (see Luke 23:43), but He was not left there. At His ascension, He led captivity captive, leaving paradise for heaven, taking with Him all its inhabitants. Now, at death, the believer goes immediately to heaven. "Absent from the body, and to be present with the Lord" (2 Cor. 5:8).

The lower section of hades, called *hell* or the "bottomless pit," contains all who die without Christ as personal Savior, and will remain in the abode of the lost until it is "cast into the lake of fire" (Rev. 20:14–15).

Surely, no other portion of Old Testament Scripture had such a soul-gripping influence in the life of Jesus as the Psalm portraying His agony and shame on the cross. That its intimate descriptive language was part of His very being is evident. The first verse of Psalm 22 constituted His cry while nailed to the tree—"My God, my God, why hast thou forsaken me?" After His resurrection, we can imagine how He would linger over this Calvary Psalm as He expounded the Psalms to His disciples (see Luke 24:44).

Among further Psalms predictive of Him who was to come as a partaker of our flesh, is Psalm 23, so eloquent of the truth associated with His Shepherd-like love, care, and provision. While in fashion as man, Jesus could relate this Psalm to Himself and declare, "I am the good shepherd: the good shepherd giveth his life for the sheep" (John 10:11). Then in Psalm 24:10, Christ had no difficulty in identifying Himself as, "The LORD of hosts, he is the King of glory."

In Isaiah, we discover that no other writer of the Old Testament records so much predictive material concerning Christ's appearance in human form. Isaiah is mentioned by name over twenty times in the Gospels. Our Lord must have had a deep personal attachment to the Book of Isaiah; He quoted from it more often than from any other prophet. Scofield has this introductory note in his *Reference Bible*—

Isaiah is justly accounted the chief of the writing prophets. He has the more comprehensive testimony and is distinctly the prophet of redemption. Nowhere else in the Scriptures written under the law have we so clear a view of grace. The New Testament Church does not appear (Eph. 3:3–10), but Messiah in His Person and sufferings, and the blessing of the Gentiles through Him, are in full vision.

It was Isaiah who gave us the prophecy of the Man Christ Jesus in His final earth-role of Judge of all nations, and as the Prince of Peace, who compels those nations to "beat their swords into plowshares, and their spears into pruninghooks" (Is. 2:4). The prophet also predicted the virgin birth of Christ, whose name would be known as *Immanuel* (see Is. 7:14), meaning "God with us," and who, as "the crown of glory" (Is. 28:5), would appear in dual form as Mary's first-born child and also as the Son of God (see Is. 9:6).

Isaiah likewise foreshadowed the coming of Jesus as "a precious corner stone, a sure foundation" (Is. 28:16) whom men would behold. As the King He will reign in righteousness, but as the man who "shall be as an hiding place from the wind, and a covert from the tempest . . . as the shadow of a great rock in a weary land" (Is. 32:2).

Further, Isaiah is the prophet who saw the coming Christ as the Servant in whom His Father delighted. He would make His appearance on earth—first as the despised, rejected, and slain Servant; second as the powerful Conqueror of nations (see Is. 42:1–4; 49:1–17). The prophet is likewise the writer who gives us a vivid description of death by crucifixion, hundreds of years before the Romans invented such a brutal practice (see Is. 50:6; 52:14).

Every verse of chapter 53 drips with the ruby blood of Jesus. This chapter opens with a reference to Him as "a root out of a dry ground" (v. 2)—which symbol reveals His Jewish stock—and then goes on to give us a prophetic portrayal of Him as the Man of Sorrows, acquainted with human grief. This description of the pain and anguish of the Cross will never be superceded.

Further, there is no more complete summary of the earthly ministry of Jesus than that given in Isaiah 61:1–2. The Master quoted it as the motto for the beginning of His ministry (see Luke 4:18–19). Attention should also be given to the foregleams of Jesus as the Intercessor, Redeemer, and Judge (see Is. 59:17).

Jeremiah, the weeping prophet, must have been another of the prophets Jesus loved to expound. Matthew saw in Jeremiah's sad picture of "Rachel weeping for her children" (Jer. 31:15), a prophecy of Herod's slaughter of the innocent babies when Christ was born. Matthew also names Jeremiah as one of the prophets Jesus was thought to be (see Matt. 16:14).

From Lamentations to Haggai there are many signposts directing us to the sufferings of Christ and the glory that should follow. If only, for example, we could have a record of what Jesus said about the mystery of the Book of Daniel, what an insight we would have into the significance of Daniel's prophecies related to Jesus!

Zechariah was the prophet who gave to the world unmistakable predictions of the coming of the Man Christ Jesus. What a presentation he cites of Him who would be born a King and who would be acclaimed as King as He rode into Jerusalem on an ass (see Zech. 9:9). Then we have a foreshadowing of the betrayal and death of Jesus, of the blood-money Judas would receive for selling his Lord, and the form of death He would die (Zech. 11:12–13; 13:6–7).

It is left to Malachi, the last of the Prophets, to indicate that John the Baptist would appear as the forerunner of Jesus. From Malachi we learn of His consequent ministry as Redeemer and Refiner, and also as the Sun of Righteousness who will arise with healing in His wings (see Mal. 3:1–3; 4:2). How the saints of old who feared the Lord often conversed with each other about the coming of their Messiah! Malachi tells that the Lord heard and recorded all they thought and said. Such devout souls, who waited for the consolation of Israel, are counted as divine jewels (see Mal. 3:17).

Between Malachi and Matthew there is a period of some 400 years known as "the silent years." We have no account from either Testament of the history of such a long period. We are given, however, a glimpse of those godly souls who, in the last century of the inter-Testament period, eagerly awaited the coming of the One to whom all past prophets gave witness.

There was the just and devout Simeon, who, inspired by the Holy Spirit, received the assurance that he would not die until he had seen the Lord's Christ. What joy was his as he took the baby Jesus up in his arms, saying that he could now die in peace for his eyes had gazed upon Him who had been born as the Savior of the world (see Luke 2:25–35).

Then there was Anna, well over 100 years of age, and, therefore, born in the last century of "the silent years," whose home was the temple and whose days were saturated with self-denial and prayers. Evidently she saw the Holy Child Jesus at the same time as Simeon, and went out to proclaim His birth to all who looked for redemption in Jerusalem (see Luke 2:36–38).

CHRIST IN THE GOSPELS

We now find ourselves in the presence of Him who became a partaker of our flesh and blood (see Heb. 2:14). An impressive fact is that as the Old Testament begins with a prophecy of the humanity of Jesus (see Gen. 3:15), so the New Testament commences with the human genealogy of the predicted One. He is heralded as "the son of David"—His royal descent (Matt. 1:1)—as "the son of Abraham" (Matt. 1:1)—His priestly descent—as the son of "Mary, of whom was born Jesus" (Matt. 1:16)—His human descent.

The Son of man's sojourn on earth was only some

thirty-three years, the first thirty being silent years lived out in an obscure, despised village. We have only one glimpse of Him during those long years, namely, when at twelve years of age, He visited the temple with His parents. Not until Jesus was thirty years of age did He appear as the Lamb of God to bear the sin of the world three years hence.

Jewish leaders, who anticipated the coming of the Messiah, rejected the hitherto unknown Man of Nazareth. Nathanael probably echoed their taunt, "Can there any good thing come out of Nazareth?" (John 1:46). The tone of contempt is also detected in the question, "Is not this the carpenter?" (Mark 6:3)—presuming an ordinary village carpenter was unqualified to be a Messiah. Yet, in the final three years of His presence on earth, the despised Galilean lived a life, preached a gospel, and died a death that transformed the history of the world.

There are three ways by which we can fully realize all that was implied in Jesus' being found in fashion as a man throughout His public ministry of some three years.

1. We see Him as a man. Prominence is given in the four Gospels to the true humanity of Jesus, who came as Mary's first-born Son. As the Eternal Son, He became the Son of man that He might make the sons of men into the sons of God. As He entered His brief but dynamic ministry, evidences abound that He became bone of our bone and flesh of our flesh.

We often sing of Him as "the sympathizing Jesus," and He was always ready to soothe and sympathize in His contact with a needy humanity. But do we distinguish as we should between *sorrow* and *sympathy*?

One can have sorrow for persons without experiencing their anguish. Sympathy, however, is the fruit of personal knowledge and experience. The very word, *sympathy,* means "a suffering with." The prophet Ezekiel was a scholar in the school of sympathy when, numbered among the captives of Chebar, he could say, "I sat where they sat" (Ezek. 3:15). It is said of Jesus that He was tried and tested as we are, yet was without sin.

As our High Priest, He is ever touched with the feeling of our infirmities, which makes Him precious to our hearts. He knows; He loves; He cares. This is why we can approach His throne of grace and find necessary help in time of need.

The following paradoxes associated with our Lord are truly amazing:

Think of it—He who was the Creator of the ends of the earth, and who fainted not, neither was weary, took upon Himself the limitations of our humanity and thus knew what it was to be weary with His journeying as He went about doing good. Sitting by the side of Jacob's well, He was grateful for the rest it provided.

Think of it—He brought the swirling waters into existence. "The sea is his, and he made it" (Ps. 95:5). Yet He knew what it was to be thirsty. He asked for a drink of water from the woman who came to draw water for her household. As Jesus died, He cried, "I thirst" (John 19:28). A soldier near the cross pressed a vinegar-soaked sponge to the dry, parched, and swollen lips of Jesus. Relieved, He uttered with a loud voice, His triumphant conquest, *"It is finished"* (John 19:30).

Think of it—He who said, "The silver is mine, and the gold is mine" (Hag. 2:8), and who was rich in His past glory, became so poor as to be born in another's home, to dine at another's table, and to be buried in another's grave. But through His poverty we are made rich.

Think of it—He who fashioned the heavens and the earth, when He entered His ministry, often knew not where to lay His head.

Think of it—He who could say, "If I were hungry, I would not tell thee" (Ps. 50:12), because the cattle on a thousand hills were His to feed upon, often hungered as a Man. He was tempted by Satan to turn stones into bread to satisfy the pangs of hunger He endured.

Think of it—He who can take His fragrant handkerchief and wipe the tears from every eye, yet came to know what it was to have a tear-stained face of His own. "Jesus wept" (John 11:35).

Think of it—He, who as the Keeper of Israel, neither slumbered nor slept, succumbed to exhaustion and fell into a deep sleep in a disciple's boat.

Think of it—He who lighted every person's coming into the world and who proclaimed Himself to be the Light of the World, yet suffered in dense darkness on the cross.

Think of it—He who knew no sin, but was "holy, harmless, undefiled, separate from sinners" (Heb. 7:26), yet became sin for sinners and died as their sinless substitute.

Think of it—He who was a Creator of all life and would declare, "I am . . . the life" (John 14:6), yet yielded up His own life and died a premature death at the age of thirty-three. The poet reminds us, "Not one hair was gray, / On His crucifixion day."

The Gospels offer many more glimpses of Him who became the Man Christ Jesus. Daily He journeyed to heal the sick, to cheer the despondent, to comfort the sorrowing. His warm, human sympathy blessed many a downcast heart. Even the little children quickly responded to His love as He took them up in His arms and blessed them.

It is said of Jesus while in human form, "Never man spake like this man" (John 7:46). All who heard His powerful sermon delivered in the temple, "wondered at the gracious words which proceeded out of his mouth" (Luke 4:22). No other man born of woman has ever captured the allegiance of millions down through the ages by what he said and taught as Jesus has.

2. We see Him as God-with-us. When Jesus appeared as Mary's first-born child, He came as God manifest in flesh, as God-with-us. In Him dwelt the fullness of the Godhead in a body (see Col. 2:9). Deity was robed undiminished with the garment of humanity. Deity and humanity were not isolated parts of His Person. They were united without confusion into one marvelous whole as Emmanuel. He is God and Man at once!

Ascending the Mount to pray, He was suddenly transfigured in the presence of Moses and Elijah and the disciples. The glorified Man manifested the momentary outflashing of Christ—inherent majesty and glory as very God of very God. Afterwards, one who gazed upon Him wrote, "We beheld his glory" (John 1:14).

Mingling His warm tears with those of the sorrowing relatives over the death of Lazarus, whom Jesus loved, He revealed a true human heart. But as God, He could command the grave to surrender its prisoner. He proclaimed, "Lazarus, come forth. And he that was dead came forth" (John 11:43–44). As the Man, Jesus knows all about our human needs; and as God, He can meet every one of them. Thus as a poet reminds us:

It is a human hand I hold,
It is a hand divine.

A most impressive fact of our Lord's brief ministry is that He never used His diety to relieve the needs of His own humanity. His Godlike power was employed only for the physical and material benefit of others. Satan urged Jesus as God to make bread out of stones to appease His hunger but without avail. At Calvary, one of the thieves, dying with Jesus, called upon Him to exercise His prerogative as God and save all three from a terrible death. "If thou be Christ, save thyself and us" (Luke 23:39). He could have made His cross a throne and smitten all His crucifiers with sudden death, but He remained nailed to the tree until He had drained life's bitter cup to its dregs.

3. We see Him as the guiltless Man dying for guilty men. Only the just are qualified to die for the unjust. When Jesus left glory for earth, He did not assume the nature of angels but the seed of Abraham for the purpose so clearly indicated in Hebrews 2:14–16. Although made in the likeness of our flesh in order to be made sin for us, He was never a sinner. He was the Lamb without spot or blemish, and ever remained "holy, harmless, undefiled, separate from sinners" (Heb. 7:26), and, therefore, the only one qualified to die as the sinless substitute for sinners. This was the purpose for which He was born to Mary as "that holy thing" (Luke 1:35).

Death came upon Jesus as the evidence and fruit of man's sin. The godly One died for the ungodly, to "taste death for every man" (Heb. 2:9). It is beyond our human comprehension that millions of human deaths could be rolled into one death and such an intolerable load borne by Him who came as the Savior of the world.

> In our place condemned He stood,
> Sealed our pardon with His blood;
> Hallelujah! What a Savior.

CHRIST IN THE ACTS, THE EPISTLES, AND THE REVELATION

The rest of the New Testament from the Acts through the Book of Revelation is heavy with the truth that, having the nature of God, Jesus took upon Himself our human nature. As can be seen in the stirring Book of Acts, it begins with the announcement that Jesus of Nazareth, renowned for His works and words while among men, had been crucified but rose again, a victor over the dark domain, and was seen alive by many saints before His ascension on high (see Acts 1:3).

Christ's departure to heaven was witnessed by His disciples, who were overwhelmed by this wonderful experience of One they had come to love and serve. They were equally amazed when two angelic announcers assured them that the very same Jesus they saw vanish would come again to receive them and all the saints unto Himself forever. Emphasis, we feel, is on the simple word *same*, which must have brought much consolation to the hearts of the disciples now that their much-loved Master was no longer with them in the flesh.

The fascinating truth is that He ascended into heaven as the glorified Man, with flesh and bones, hands and feet, and is alive forever more (see Luke 24:39–40). Equally soul-gripping is the revelation that, when He returns to gather His saints, He will come just as He is—"the Lord *himself*" (1 Thess. 4:16, italics added), to bring them into an unbreakable, eternal union with Himself (see John 14:3). On the glorious day of *Pentecost*, the Spirit of Christ made His promised return—a prominent, practical, and activating motive in the life and service of the apostles.

The angel-faced Stephen's cruel martyrdom for Christ's sake brought its reward in at least two directions. First, the Spirit-filled martyr, as he was being stoned to death, looked not on his murderers but steadfastly toward heaven and saw both "the glory of God and Jesus standing on the right hand of God" (Acts

7:55). At His ascension, entering heaven, we are specifically informed that Jesus "sat down on the right hand of the Majesty on high" (Heb. 1:3).

While the difference of posture is given, there is no contradiction whatever between Jesus *standing* and *seated*. The truth implied is that as Jesus watched His heroic servant Stephen dying such a terrible death on His behalf and about to enter heaven praying, "Lord Jesus, receive my spirit" (Acts 7:59), the Lord Himself rose from His throne-seat and stood waiting to give His martyred follower a royal welcome as he entered the pearly gates.

The stoning of Stephen, however, had another remarkable result. One who witnessed the terrible death was Saul of Tarsus who, as the persecutor of the church, was responsible for the imprisonment and death of many early saints. He heard Stephen pray as he died, "Lord, lay not this sin to their charge" (Acts 7:60). Thereafter, Saul could not erase from his mind the victorious death of Stephen. It was while Saul was on his mission of slaughtering the saints that the miracle happened that transformed *Saul*, the archenemy of the church, into *Paul*, "the apostle extraordinary."

Suddenly, on the road to Damascus, Saul found himself enveloped in heavenly light. He heard a heavenly voice asking, "Why persecutest thou Me?" (Acts 9:4).

Asking who the speaker was, the avowed enemy of the church received the reply, "I am Jesus whom thou persecutest" (Acts 9:5). The Bible student asks how Saul could persecute Jesus when He was in heaven and the truth emerges that Jesus and His own are one. That which affects the members of His body is felt by Him who is its head. It was Jesus of Nazareth who brought about the dramatic transformation of Saul, fashioning him into a chosen vessel for the salvation of Gentiles and the most prolific writer in the New Testament (see Acts 9:15).

Paul's matchless Epistles prove that Jesus, made in fashion as a man, became a living, bright Reality. Now, the Man in yonder glory became the center in all things in the life and labors of the apostle. Paul gave the church an insight into not only the death and resurrection of Jesus but also into His present heavenly ministry. The past humiliation and present glorification of the Master Paul dearly loved and devotedly served was a precious theme he delighted to proclaim (see Phil. 2:5–11).

Raphael, the renowned artist, set about reading the New Testament so that he might more correctly depict the face of Jesus on canvas. Suddenly discovering the spiritual glory of His divine character, he exclaimed, "My God! My God!" Such was the experience of Paul who unfolds for us the present heavenly mediatory function of the Man Christ Jesus (see 1 Tim. 2:5; Gal. 3:19–20). In the days of His flesh, Jesus Himself has affirmed this particular office. Paul corroborates the truth that, apart from Christ, man has no access to God (see John 14:6). If it was Paul who wrote the anonymous Epistle to the Hebrews (as I believe he did, basing my view on the last section of the Epistle, Hebrews 13:18–25) then in it the apostle further emphasizes the mediatory work of the Lord Jesus (see Heb. 8:6).

It is most profitable to trace in what capacities Jesus continues His ministry in heaven and will yet function when He returns to earth. Had He not appeared on earth as Man and lived the complex life of a human being, there would never have been Christianity and the church, and He would never have been qualified to represent us, as our Forerunner, Advocate, Mediator, and Intercessor (see Heb. 5:7–10; 6:20; 7:25; 1 John 2:1).

John reminds us that when Jesus, the Eternal Word,

was made flesh and lived among men that the disciples beheld His glory, the glory as the only begotten of the Father, full of grace and truth (see John 1:14; 17:21). Paul also revelled in declaring what Christ became after He was received up into glory.

What is the practical conclusion of our meditation on the complete humanity of Him who was born of a woman? Is it not the truth that one of the marvels of eternity is that He who was made in the likeness of sinful flesh is the One who still wears our nature and has a heart beating in union with our own?

Therefore, when the cares, needs, trials, and problems of our mortal life press in upon us, we can turn to Jesus who is ever with us and for us. He ever hears our prayers, checks our fears, deals with our grievances, sympathizes with us in our sorrows and separations, and acts in every way as our Friend—even as a Friend sticking closer than a brother. He is our Great High Priest, who was tested and tried in all points like as we are and who is, therefore, touched with the experience of our infirmities (see Heb. 4:14–16). Let us remember that:

> In every pang that rends the heart,
> The Man of Sorrows shares a part.

What a blessed affirmation closes the sacred Book, taken up from the commencement to conclusion with the condescension of the God who became Man and who lived and died among men! Here it is: "And they shall see his face" (Rev. 22:4).

The inspired writers of both Old and New Testaments have painted for you and me a marvelous portrait. Nothing could be more wondrous than this picture except for the actual face of Christ. When we see Him, we shall be like Him; for we shall see Him as He is, the glorified Man Christ Jesus. Tennyson enshrines this blissful moment for us in his memorable poem, the last verse of which reads:

> For though from out our bourne of time and place
> The flood may bear me far,
> I hope to see my Pilot face to face
> When I have crossed the bar.

3

The Chiefest
Among Ten Thousand

Compare a gem to a common rock. You have no doubt about its value.

People who saw Jesus in the flesh should have had little trouble assessing His value. They merely had to compare Him to the false messiahs or to the chief priests or to thousands of people struggling to live holy lives. Eleven of the disciples recognized His value.

Judas sold his Master for thirty pieces of silver, which was the market price for a common slave. Since that betrayal, many in the world sadly undervalue the Lord Jesus Christ.

Two passages of Scripture, however, in their combination, depict His value. "Thou art worth ten thousand of us" (2 Sam. 18:3), declared the Israelites as they persuaded David not to go out to battle. The second reference is the evaluation of a lover. "My beloved is . . . the chiefest among ten thousand," (Song 5:10), replied the bride in answer to the question of the daughters of Jerusalem.

A GALLANT WARRIOR

The first reference extols David's worth. This king of Israel is one of the most magnificent characters in Holy Writ. The stories of his career never lose their charm and grip for young or old. But the Bible, true to life, tells the truth of each life. It portrays the defects as well as the glories of a reign like David's. In its pages we find him suffering the consequences of his dark sin. In fleeing from Absalom, he was but reaping what he had sown.

The verse about his worth, however, provides us with a beautiful touch in an otherwise sad story. It reveals the love and loyalty of those who followed David. To them, he was worth ten thousand of the best. There was none like him. Such admiration brought comfort to his broken heart. His followers encouraged their king to stay behind and succor, guide, and bless those who remained. If he were killed in battle, then their light would be quenched. Because of his kingly qualities, David's place could not be filled by any other.

Was he not Israel's brave leader and king? Had he not been divinely anointed as their sovereign? Was he not a man after God's own heart? To the Israelites, David was a mighty victor; and to the Philistines, a source of constant terror.

And was he not willing to suffer with his people? His own example, he believed, was better than precept; his actions, better than words. "I will surely go forth with you myself also" (2 Sam. 18:2). A commander always inspires courage when he cries, "Follow me!"

Yes, and was he not merciful and considerate? Absalom, his wayward son, was the cause of his anguish. Absalom wanted David killed! David desired Absalom spared! "Deal gently for my sake with the young man" (2 Sam. 18:5). What true magnanimity! Anticipating a

New Testament precept, David overcame evil with good.

Again, was he not loving and forgiving? David carried no revenge against his rebellious son. "Would God I had died for thee, O Absalom" (2 Sam. 18:33). When the people saw such noble traits exhibited in the daily life of their king, what else could they say but, "Thou art worth ten thousand of us" (2 Sam 18:3)?

THE ULTIMATE LOVE

The estimation in which David was held is sweetly suggestive of the Lord Jesus. This thought brings us to the typical features of a related Scripture. Israel's illustrious king is an outstanding type of the King eternal. Let us look at the statements again:

"Thou art worth ten thousand of us" (2 Sam. 18:3).

"My beloved . . . is the chiefest among ten thousand" (Song 5:10).

Is there any connection between the two statements? Solomon, who wrote the second one, knew all about Israel's estimation and admiration of his father, David. And, remembering all that those brave men had said of David, Solomon placed such language in the mouth of the bride as she extols her beloved. Her beloved excelled that of many others—thousands, in fact.

Dedicated Christians may discover in such language the superior worth of our adorable Lord. They can give reasons. They know that their Savior surpasses others in many ways. For example, Christ is:

1. *Holier in birth.* Although He condescended to become the Man Christ Jesus, let it not be forgotten that He never occupied our weakness in regard to sin. There is a great gulf between His entrance into the world and ours. Being conceived of the Holy Ghost, He came into

humanity supernaturally. We were born in sin and shaped in iniquity. We came into the world by the way of natural generation. Not so Christ! If our Redeemer were not miraculously born, His value would be reduced. He would not be worth ten thousand of us, but only one of us, if His birth were not virgin. We believe, however, that He is worth a multitude of sin-born souls, in that His birth surpassed the laws of life—born of the Holy Spirit (see Luke 1:26–38).

2. *Purer in life.* The nearer a person gets to God, the more evident his or her sins become. One of the saintliest of men of the last century was Robert Murray McCheyne. Because of his eminent holiness, he has been described as "a modern saint." Yet his *Memoirs* are full of confessions of sins. Upon every page there is a fresh discovery of his evil heart! Subscribing to the experience of another, McCheyne could sing,

> They who fain would serve Thee best
> Are conscious most of sin within.

But no such confession ever left the faultless lips of the Lord Jesus! Listen again to his own claim, "Which of you convinceth [convicts] me of sin?" (John 8:46). "The prince of this world cometh, and hath nothing in me" (John 14:30). The devil, however, has something even in the best people, namely their old, evil, condemned nature.

Jesus never sinned. True, Christ has two distinct natures, combining both Deity and humanity in one person. Yet in both natures He possesses the same attribute: holiness. Therefore, He is unlike us.

Think of the holiest man you have ever heard or read about, or the saintliest woman you have ever met, and then compare such with the unsullied life of the Lord Jesus! Why, it is like holding a candle to the sun! All pale before Him, seeing He is separate from sinners, and, therefore, unmatched and incomparable. Truly, His worth is ten thousand times ten thousand that of the godliest saints who ever breathed. He is the purest of the mightiest of the pure.

Some noble souls revere the Savior and point others to Him. Such a witness was the preacher, Samuel Rutherford. After an English merchant had heard Rutherford preach at St. Andrew's, he said, "I heard a little fair man, and he showed me the *loveliness of Christ.*"

Rutherford lived and loved to exalt his Lord. "No pen, no worth, no image can express to you the loveliness of my only, only Lord Jesus," he wrote in one of his letters.

Yes, and it is His passion to make us like Himself. He greatly desires our purity. He waits to impart his own lovely holiness. Shall we by faith receive it?

3. *Firmer in friendship.* King David was willing to suffer with his loyal people, but responding to their considerate words, he remained behind in a safe place. Christ, however, not only reflected the words of King David, "I will surely go forth with you myself also" (2 Sam. 18:2)—He went! He suffered Himself to be tested in all points like we are.

Jesus did not call His followers slaves or servants, but friends (see John 15:15). The beauty of His friendship is seen in that He shares all our experiences, sin excepted. As the Brother born for adversity, He is with us in all the conflicts of life. All of us have friends who are kind, generous, and self-sacrificing; but the Lord Jesus is worth ten thousand of the best friends it is possible to have. The best of earth can fail, but Christ is constant, firm, abiding, changeless, and true in His friendship, love, and sympathy.

What do you know about the undying friendship of

this Friend who sticketh closer than a brother? Is He your Friend? Consider again the words of Rutherford:

> Oh, pity for evermore that there should be such an one as Christ Jesus, so boundless, so bottomless, and so incomparable in infinite excellency and sweetness, and so few to take Him! O ye poor dry and dead souls, why will ye not come hither with your toom (empty) vessels and your empty souls to this huge, and fair, and deep, and sweet well of life, and fill all your toom vessels? Oh, that Christ should be so large in sweetness and worth, and we so narrow, pinched, so ebb, and so void will not take Him! They lose their love miserably, who will not bestow it upon this lovely One.

Saintly Rutherford bestowed his love upon this lovely One. Do you?

4. *Kinder in grace.* In David's concern over Absalom, we can see a similarity to the Savior's mercy over the wayward and rebellious. The forgiving grace of Israel's king is a faint type of the loving-kindness of David's greater Son and Lord. Earth possesses a few Christians who are gracious, kind, and forgiving, who bear no revenge, carry no animosity, although despised and rejected. But Christ exceeds and excels them all! There is no love and grace like unto His. He is peerless in the realms of mercy, pardon, and forgiveness. "How shall I give thee up, Ephraim?" (Hos. 11:8). The Lord Jesus is worth ten thousand of us in that He forgives so freely. We have reserves. If a friend grieves us, we say, "Well, I will forgive him, but . . ." The Lord Jesus had no "buts." The old score is not only forgiven; it is forgotten!

No wonder Samuel Rutherford exclaimed:

> I find Christ to be Christ, and that He is far, far, even infinite heaven's height above man. And that is all our happiness. Sinners can do nothing but make wounds that Christ may heal them; and make debts that He may

pay them; and make falls, that He may raise them; and make deaths, that He may quicken them; and spin out and dig hells to themselves, that He may ransom them!

5. *Greater in sacrifice.* It was David's sorrowful lament that he was not able to die for Absalom, his son. And, although a fearless warrior, he was not allowed to fight with his brave men. The marvel of the Cross, however, is that the Lord Jesus did fight and die. He gave Himself for rebellious Absalom and every other rebel of Adam's race. David stayed behind in a safe place, but the Lord Jesus came out of His ivory palaces, and, at Calvary, achieved a glorious victory over sin and Satan.

Yes, and multitudes have died for Him. Think of the illustrious roll of martyrs, missionaries, and saints who have laid down their lives for His sake—even in the present decade! Think of the thousands who are ready, like Barnabas and Paul, to hazard their lives for the name of the Lord Jesus Christ! But His death is worth ten thousand such glorious deaths, simply because of its object. Christ died to reconcile man to God. He "died for us, that . . . we should live" (1 Thess. 5:10). In the death of the brave there may be inspiration, but in the death of the Beloved there is redemption.

6. *Higher in honor.* The funerals of John Kennedy, Charles deGaulle, and Princess Grace brought together leaders from around the world. When we think of the most honorable of earth with its kings, queens, lords, ladies, elite, noble, wise, talented, and cultured, our hearts are stirred with curiosity—and sometimes envy—and occasionally humility. But where is nobility comparable to Christ's? Is He not worth ten thouand of the highest, noblest, and most well-bred of the land? As the King of Kings, and Lord of Lords, is He not high over all? Oh, let us exalt his Person, worth, and honor!

"Who is like unto thee?" (Ex. 15:11). Let us say unto souls of men, *"Behold your God!"* Let us make much of Him, for He is ever precious to those who believe!

To adoring hearts, the Savior is the Star of brightest splendor. What is He worth to you? To me, He is the chiefest and fairest of all the earth beside, seeing that it is to His love and grace I owe all that I am and have. "God hath made many fair flowers," wrote Rutherford, "but the fairest of them all is heaven, and the flower of all flowers is Christ."

The psalmist's confession was, "Whom have I in heaven but thee? and there is none upon earth that I desire beside thee" (Ps. 73:25). And, to quote dear old Samuel Rutherford again, "Sure I am He is the far best half of heaven, yea, He is all heaven, and more than all heaven."

I have written these words to change your life. You have studied how people evaluated their warrior King or how a holy woman prized her lover—worth "ten thousand" (2 Sam. 18:3) and "the chiefest" among them (Song 5:10). Your estimation of Christ can be judged by the value you place upon His friendship. Consider the position you give Him in your life. Worship and witness are ever the test of worth. He *is* the chiefest, but do you give Him the chiefest place? "Christians," Dr. J. Stuart Holden tells us in *The Pre-eminent Lord*, "are mainly divisible into three classes—those who give Him *place*, those who give Him *prominence*, and those who give Him *pre-eminence*." Are you giving Him the best?

A witness who showed a merchant the loveliness of Christ said, "Every day we see some new thing in Christ. His love hath neither brim nor bottom."

Is Rutherford's experience ours? Listen to him again!

Christ all the seasons of the year is dropping sweetness;
if I had vessels I might fill them, but my old riven, holey,

and running-out dish, even when I am at the well, can bring little away. Nothing but glory will make tight and fast our leaking and rifty vessels. . . . How little of the sea can a child carry in his hand; as little do I take away of my great sea, my boundless and running-over Christ Jesus.

What a beautiful description this is of the all-sufficiency and pre-eminence of the Master! "The boundless and running-over Christ Jesus." May ours be the appropriation of His fullness, and the undying passion to give Him the place of pre-eminence in all things!

He stands forth, does He not, upon the highest principle of heavenly glory, proclaimed by God as His eternal Son, acknowledged by angels, adored by saints, and feared by Satan and his evil hosts. He is the living and mighty Christ, our Savior and Lord, the world's master Teacher, Preacher, Warrior, Friend, the fairest of ten thousand, and the ultimate Love.

4

The Center and
Circumference of All Things

Most people, it seems, in our cynical and secular age put possessions, power, and pleasure above everything else. Some of them will acknowledge the church building with an occasional visit and Christ with an occasional reference to His teachings. Is this enough for Him?

Christless eyes see no beauty in Jesus that they should desire Him, but true faith acknowledges Him to be the Center and Sum of all things.

The purpose of the Epistle to the Colossians is to prove the pre-eminence of our Lord in every realm. It has pleased the Father to cause all fullness to reside in His beloved Son: "That in all things He might have the preeminence" (Col. 1:18).

CHRIST AND THEOLOGY

Christ is pre-eminent in Scripture. Old and New Testaments exist to reveal Him. Martin Luther said, "There is one Book and one Person. The Book is the Bible: And the Person is Jesus Christ." And the Book exalts the Person! Every part of the sacred volume reflects His blessed Person. Consider Psalm 40:7—"In the volume of the book it is written of me." He, Himself, never wrote a book, yet no library in the land could contain all the literature written about Him.

Christ is also pre-eminent in creation. He is the Creator and Sustainer of all the rolling spheres. Creation is His child! And He it is who upholds all things by the word of His power. Even though you know that He made a beautiful rosebud, you do not claim—as the pantheists do—that He is contained in that flower.

Christ is likewise pre-eminent in grace. In such a realm, He is supreme, peerless, incomparable. The saved soul sings: "There is none like unto Thee as Savior and Keeper." His grace is sufficient at all times and under all circumstances. He is the Source of every precious blessing.

The truth of our Lord's pre-eminence has been realized and revered by the greatest minds in every age and in every sphere. If He is not Lord of all, He is not Lord *at* all. He claims the recognition and admiration of the highest and the lowest. He is the magnetic attraction to which the point of the human needle flies.

CHRIST AND SCHOLARSHIP

As a child, Jesus astounded the religious leaders. As an adult, He caused the wise men of the schools to marvel at His knowledge (see John 7:14–15). If He lived today, He would be looked upon by the leaders of many a denomination as an unaccredited minister. Having never passed through a particular seminary or divinity school, He could not expect to receive official endorsement.

Jesus was not the product of the educational centers of His time. He never spent long weary years at the feet of some master. I presume that at about the age of fifteen, Jesus left school and went to labor at the carpenter's bench. He followed this trade until He was thirty years of age.

Yet, although He was no scholar after the rabbinical order, His teachings have never been fully penetrated. His wisdom was from above, and, consequently, has won the greatest intellects. He never founded a college, but all the schools together could not boast of having as many scholars as have sat at His feet. Yes, and His gospel is the greatest educative force in the world. The pioneers of modern education were sincere Christians who sat at the feet of the Master. As the Light, He banishes all error and ignorance. Once the heathen come to know Him, they want to know how to read and write.

Do you sometimes consider yourself ignorant, uneducated, and lacking brilliant gifts? Then keep near to the Christ. Ask for wisdom, as James 1:5 teaches. Are you clever, versatile, eminently gifted, polished, and blessed with all that the finest of schools can give? Then remember that you are only a polished pagan without Christ as your Savior. Let Him take your intellect and use every power as He may choose!

CHRIST AND AUTHORSHIP

Some have an urge to write. Printer's ink seems to be in their blood, and they are never happy until and unless they see themselves in print. Not so Jesus! We have no record that He ever penned a word for posterity. He allowed others to gather up His precious sayings and put them into permanent form. Only once are we told that Jesus wrote anything. That was when He scratched a condemning message in the dust—a message bringing conviction to the men who accused a woman of adultery. Because it was written in the dust, He could easily obliterate it after it had achieved its purpose.

Not so long ago $14,000 was paid for a few leaves of *Pickwick Papers*. How much more would we give for a few words in the handwriting of Jesus? They would be counted among the world's greatest treasures. But here is the marvel—although Jesus never wrote an Epistle, as did some of His apostles, His sayings have been translated into over one thousand languages, and new tongues are captured continually for the proclamation of His redeeming gospel.

Think of the countless thousands of theological and devotional books His spoken words have inspired! An outstanding American religious writer proudly showed me his library of seven thousand books, all of which were about Christ and His Word. I was impressed with his collection. But what are these among so many? My friend has only a very small section of the world's volumes centering around our Lord. Truly, they seem as numberless as the sand on the seashore! And after over nineteen hundred years, the output of the religious writers on the Person and influence of the Savior reveal a staggering total.

Call to mind the numberless sermons and messages His words daily inspire. Take one city alone. Count up all its ministers, Sunday school teachers, evangelists, and Christian workers who speak about Jesus in all kinds of meetings, and you will discover what a perennial topic He is. Yet, He was cradled in poverty and reared in obscurity.

CHRIST AND ART

Certainly the pre-Incarnate Christ was the Creator of all beauty and color. In Creation, He displayed His artistry. He it was who colored the flowers with their beautiful tints and who formed the marvelous landscapes, which artists strive to represent. And His fingers are still responsible for the glorious sunsets and the matchless rainbow. These blessings of beauty cause you to praise Him.

What pictures He could have painted! What colors He could have used! The wonder, however, is that although He never used a brush and palette, He has inspired all the great masterpieces in the realm of art. The master artists of the past—Raphael, Leonardo da Vinci, Michelangelo, El Greco, and others—were all captivated by the thought and vision of Christ. And so precious are their works that fortunes are paid when one bcomes available.

CHRIST AND ARCHITECTURE

He was the great Architect of the universe. He it was who formed the starry heavens and fashioned the worlds with all their marvels, and hung the earth in space. Every part of our planet, as well as every part of life upon it, reveals a wonderful forethought and perfect construction. Plan and order are everywhere! His master mind can be seen in the formation and in the properties of a blade of grass.

While He lived on earth, Jesus was so poor that He possessed no home of His own. Foxes could tunnel their holes, and the birds could build their nests; but for the Master, there was nowhere to lay His head. He never made a house for Himself, as Solomon did. He lived in borrowed houses. When there was no one to welcome Him, He sought the covering roof of the star-lit sky above.

Yet, what miracles He could have performed! With a gesture, He could have fashioned for Himself a beautiful palace—just as easily and as quickly as He caused the gourd to grow for Jonah's protection. If it were possible for Him to raise the temple of His body in three days, what a magnificent stone structure He could have erected! But He never placed one stone upon another. Having power to rear gorgeous temples out of rubbish, He was content to move among people, building on their consciences and loyalties, yet He knew His work was more permanent than the architect's or mason's.

Once again, however, we discover His uniqueness. Although He didn't build a home for Himself, the greatest cathedrals in the world were erected for the worship of His name. Some of them took centuries to complete. The stately structures of Milan, Cologne, St. Paul's, Canterbury, or other locations all exist that hundreds of adoring worshipers might gather at His feet. Crowning the vast majority of European cathedrals or American rural churches is the figure of His cross, out of which the church was born. The death-throes of Calvary were the birth-throes of the church!

CHRIST AND POETRY

Jesus, the Word of God, possessed the poetic gift. Otherwise His Spirit would never had inspired those incomparable poems of the Old Testament. And the gracious words leaving His lips also proved that grace had been poured into them. No man spoke as this Man!

Yet He never created a poem for His followers to recite. With the most perfect of all voices—tender, strong, and capable of all inflection what heart-moving poems He could have produced and recited. The simplicity, beauty, and charm of His language indicate His capabilities.

Strange, is it not, that although He never left a poem, the greatest poetic productions revolve around His Person? The world's master poets dipped their pens in the ink of love to Christ. When you study Milton, Shakespeare, Browning, Tennyson, Whittier, and a hundred lesser lights in the poetic world, you will find that their most soul-inspiring lines are those fragrant with the thought of Christ!

CHRIST AND MUSIC

We have only one record of the Man of Sorrows' singing. Even then His voice was mingled with others. He was one of the male-voice choir that sang as He went out to His cross. When they—Christ and His disciples—had sung a hymn, they went out. And sing, Jesus could, seeing that He was anointed with the oil of gladness above His fellows. But with the melody of heaven in His soul, we are not told that He played an instrument like David of old. Yet He must love beautiful music. After all, the morning stars sang together, and He has an orchestra of harps and harpists in heaven.

But although Jesus left no song behind, He has inspired all the soul-thrilling oratorios of our master musicians. The creations of Handel, Bach, Beethoven, and Mendelssohn, pulsate with praise to our adorable Lord. The most sublime music we possess has come from hearts touched by the Christ who is responsible for all melody and harmony. And of this we are confident, that the grand "new song" He is creating for us to sing will surpass the most appealing rhapsodies of earth.

CHRIST AND SOCIAL REFORM

Ardent socialists claim Jesus as One whose message and methods were communistic and revolutionary. What proof do they have? He wanted to be called "Teacher." He never called Himself a revolutionary. He was no enemy of a constitutional order of things. He urged citizens to render unto Caesar the things that were Caesar's. Christ did not concentrate upon the betterment of man's outward conditions. His work was deeply spiritual. "Repent ye" (Mark 1:15) and "Ye must be born again" (John 3:7) were basic. He saw that individual lives needed converting. Jesus' power was certainly radical, even revolutionary, but it was always spiritual in its nature. Socialists want better conditions. Jesus knew that better hearts had to occur before people could expect better conditions.

Yet the marvel is that His gospel creates a social conscience. Christianity is the mightiest social force the world has ever known. Whenever and wherever Christ's precepts are taught and obeyed, industrial and communal problems are quickly solved. Hatred, greed, selfishness, slavery, wretched inequality, and the denial of another's rights can never live in the light of His countenance. Where Jesus reigns, there righteousness occupies the thoughts and actions of all concerned.

CHRIST AND WEALTH

In His own right, He is Owner of all. It was He who placed all the silver, gold, and precious jewels into the casket of the earth. The cattle upon a thousand hills are His. The earth with its fullness is His. If hungry He would tell no man, seeing that the world with its bountiful store was His pantry.

The mystery wrapped up in His incarnation, however, was that although He was rich, for our sakes He became poor. And how poor He was! He was born in a stall and entered upon a life of voluntary poverty. He actually borrowed a penny in order to enforce a lesson on paying taxes and the giving to God of His dues. When He died, He left nothing behind save His mother and His cross. Mary sought shelter in the borrowed home of John, while His cross of anguish was what He bequeathed to a lost world.

Fortunes have been flung at the feet of Him who, in His poverty, dined at another man's table. Think of the surrender that dedicated Christians of the past were willing to make for Christ's sake! Think of the consecrated sacrifices of believers in all parts of the world! Willingly men and women bring their silver and their gold that such may be used in His happy service. He it is who guides the giving of multitudes that His cause might be maintained. Hospitals, colleges, mission stations result. From the woman with her alabaster jar of ointment to a Nobel prize-winner giving away a fortune, Jesus inspires giving. He is worthy of our last penny.

CHRIST AND HOME

The world gave Him a cold reception. There was no room for Him—the One for whom every family is named—in the inn. When He stepped out into His ministry, it was to hear the click of closing doors on every hand. He lived and died as the unwanted One. His own, we are told, received Him not. We can guess that on more than one occasion, after listening to His message, the people would retire to their homes and forget Jesus. Possibly on more than one night, He found His way to the Mount of Olives where, with darkness as

His blanket and the green grass as His bed, He would snatch what sleep He could.

Yet, it is the homeless Christ who creates the Christian home. He it is who secures its safety and sanctity. Home life reaches its zenith when He is recognized as Head. There is beauty all around when His love is at home. Degraded home life today—with all its sad divisions, shocking child abuse, teen-age rebellion, lovelessness, and tragedy of divorce—needs Jesus. One poet speaks of "home" as heaven's fallen sister. When Christ takes up His abode in any home, it becomes heaven's outpost. What place has He in your home? If you want a happy home, let Him occupy the throne.

Because of their acquaintance with suffering and sensitivity to feeling, women were drawn to Him and ministered to Him. The last person He spoke to was a woman, and the first to hear His voice after His resurrection was a woman. Women had no hand in his cruel death.

Once He passed beyond His mother's care, He had no woman at His side to cheer, encourage, and inspire as only a good woman can. Yet womanhood owes its high calling to Him. Where His name is not known, woman is the slave or drudge of man. Generally speaking, women seem more religious than men and are to be found in greater numbers in many congregations. Their devotion is a tribute to Jesus as Emancipator. He gives the truest kind of liberation. His cross is the charter of woman's freedom.

Christ had no child, someone said, that He might adopt all children. Homeless and wifeless, He did not have the recognition of a baby's smile, so precious to the heart of a parent. Yet, this is the One who loved and was loved by children. He it was who taught the world to prize and value the child. "Suffer the little children to come unto me" (Mark 10:14) was His message to those who sought to keep the little feet from running to Him.

Think of the way in which the child is surrounded with holy and wholesome influences as the result of His gospel. The mothers of Jerusalem brought their children to His arms to be blessed, and mothers today are delivered from fear when they know that young people have a conscious experience of the Savior's grace. And when we observe what a marvelous power our Sunday schools have over the lives of children, how we praise God for Jesus! In the days of His flesh He taught His disciples many precious lessons from babes and sucklings. Thank God for homes built on the foundation stone of Christ.

Yes, beloved, we have a wonderful Christ. Truly, there is none like Him! He is our never-failing treasury filled with boundless stores of grace. How heart-stirring and satisfying are our glimpses of Christ, who is high over all. The Master we love and serve is peerless, matchless, incomparable. He has no equal.

The question we must honestly face, however, is the one concerning His supremacy over our life. Supreme as He is in every other realm, we can forbid His reigning over the little empire of the heart. Do we give Him the place of pre-eminence in all things? Have we brought forth the royal diadem and crowned Him Lord of our time, talents, and treasures? If not, then may the gracious Holy Spirit prompt you to make this prayer your own:

> In all my heart and will, Lord Jesus,
>   Be altogether King.
> Make me Thy loyal subject, Lord Jesus,
>   To Thee in everything.

5

The Three in One

In this chapter of our study, let us seek to trace the mystic union between the Father, Son, and Holy Spirit. The Bible reveals a wonderful intimacy between Christ and the Holy Spirit. Remember how He said: "I . . . by the Spirit of God" (Matt. 12:28). That relationship characterizes not only the casting out of demons but our Lord's every action. For His life was saturated through and through with the presence and power of the Holy Spirit. His human frame became the mystic cabinet of the Third Person of the blessed Trinity.

When the Lord Jesus left heaven, He became absolutely subordinate to the Father and dependent upon the Holy Spirit. Although He was fully God and fully man, He declared that, apart from the Father, He could do nothing. And in the phrase quoted above you have His dependence as well on the Spirit of God. In this He has left us an example, that we should follow in His steps. We can only be fruitful in our service for the Lord as, like the Master, we are subordinate to the Father and dependent upon the Holy Spirit.

The next thought, which possibly may be new to you, is this: When our Lord was here on the earth, it would seem as if the Holy Spirit exclusively limited Himself to the Lord Jesus Christ. Have you ever noticed this in the study of the Gospels: After our Lord's wondrous birth by the Holy Spirit, we have no reference to the Spirit of God's being related to any other individual until our Lord, after His resurrection, breathed upon His disciples and said, "Receive ye the Holy Ghost" (John 20:22)? I have searched the Gospels and tried to find some reference, and I cannot trace any at all. And so it would seem that the Holy Spirit exclusively empowered the Lord Jesus in the days of His earthly life.

This may explain the inspired words in John 7:39: "The Holy Ghost was not yet given." There had to be a Man who could receive the Holy Spirit in His fullness ere that fullness could be bestowed upon man. And for the first time, in the Lord Jesus, there was One well able to receive the Holy Spirit in His totality. And then, on the day of Pentecost, the Lord Jesus sent the Holy Spirit as His ascension gift to His believing people. And now it is possible for any child of God to be filled with the Holy Spirit, for in Jesus He fills a person. Thus the gospel exhibits a beautiful blending, uniting, merging, infusing, wonderful to behold.

PROPHESIED BY THE SPIRIT

1 Peter 1:11

The apostle tells us the Holy Spirit was in the prophets, testifying beforehand the sufferings of Christ and the glory that should follow. You can add to that, if you like, 2 Peter 1:20–21, where he tells us the holy men of old wrote as they were moved by the Holy Spirit. This brings us to the wonderful truth that in the Old Testament, the Holy Spirit was preparing the way for the Lord Jesus.

We are told by some superficial theologians in these days that we can do without the Old Testament; if we have the New, they claim, that is sufficient. But you cannot understand the New if you do not have the Old. And the word of Peter sets the seal of authenticity upon the Old Testament. If the Old Testament was inspired of the Holy Spirit, then we cannot and we dare not be without it.

We refer to John the Baptist as the forerunner of Jesus, and so he was. But the Holy Spirit was the Divine forerunner of Jesus. For He it was who in the Old Testament prepared the way for Jesus. So when Jesus appeared among men He could lay hold of Old Testament Scriptures and relate them to Himself, "of whom Moses in the law, and the prophets, did write" (John 1:45). So in types and symbols and in the experiences of the people of God as they journeyed through the wilderness and in history and poetry and prophecy, you have the way prepared for Jesus.

Then as the time drew near for our Lord's birth, the Holy Spirit was especially active in the minds of one or two godly souls. For example, in Luke 1:67, we read that Zachariah was filled with the Holy Spirit, and made a distinct prophecy regarding the coming Savior. In Luke 2:25, the Holy Ghost contacted the mind of Simeon. It was revealed unto him by the Holy Spirit that he should not die until he had seen the Lord's Christ.

Just as the Holy Spirit prepared the way for the first coming of Jesus, I have the conviction that in these last days the same blessed Spirit, "the promise of my Father" (Luke 24:49), is preparing the way for the Second Coming of Jesus. He is preparing God's own people.

Yes, He is preparing the world for the Second Advent of Christ.

BORN OF THE HOLY SPIRIT

Matthew 1:18

Mary, overshadowed by the Most High, was found with child of the Holy Spirit. Here we find ourselves in the presence of the mystery of the Holy Trinity. We need to look to the Lord for fitting language as we come to express this most sacred truth. You remember the words of Job: "How can he be clean that is born of a woman?" (Job 25:4). Our Lord was born of a woman; yet He was clean. Our Lord was born of a sinful woman; yet He emerged with a sinless body. Mary recognized that she was a sinner. She confessed her need of a Savior. "My spirit hath rejoiced in God my Savior" (Luke 1:47). Yet, although Mary was a sinful woman, she gave birth to One who was sinless. You cannot explain the sinlessness of Jesus apart from His wonderful birth.

What happened in the incarnation of our Lord? The Holy Spirit came upon the virgin's womb, where the body of Jesus was to be formed. He purified it as the chemist purifies the metal. The divine seed was planted there. This is the implication of the phrase, "that holy thing which shall be born of thee" (Luke 1:35) "The holy thing" refers to the sinless person of Jesus.

To me, this explains why Christ did not sin. Never forget that Jesus Christ brought with Him from the glory of His Father, the divine nature. He came as God, and as God he hated sin. Not only so, but Jesus was born with a sinless humanity.

We were born in sin and shapen in iniquity, but our Lord brought with Him, as God, His own sinlessness. He added to that his sinless humanity.

You may say, "If Jesus could not sin, then there was no

point at all in the temptations. What was the purpose of the temptations if there was no liability in Him to sin?" The answer is this: Jesus presented Himself to hell as well as to earth as the sinless one, and the devil was not going to let that claim pass unchallenged. Hence the significance of the temptation. And Jesus went through the wilderness and was tempted in all points like as we are, yet without sin. He emerged blessedly victorious.

Now when Satan comes to us, he has something to which to appeal. He has a little bit of territory in each one of us in the sense of our union with Adam's fallen race—our sinful nature. He did not hold that territory in Jesus, the Second Adam. Jesus was born the sinless progenitor of a new race! There were no evil propensities in the humanity of our Lord. He emerged with a sinless life, owing to His miraculous conception and His Spirit-led determination.

Here is a blessed truth of Holy Writ: When the devil comes to us and seeks to exercise authority over us because of his victory over Adam, we too can be blessedly victorious. The Holy Spirit is within us to apply the victory of our Lord. Greater is He that is in us than he that is in the world.

And further, we must not forget this fact as we think of the wondrous birth of our Lord: In the Incarnation, the Holy Spirit completed the union between deity and humanity. God the Father through the Holy Spirit sent the Lord Jesus as God and as man. The Lord Jesus was not part God and part man. He was the God-man, fully able to save. In the Incarnation, the Holy Spirit added to our Lord's existent divine nature, a human nature.

In our new birth the reverse happens. The Holy Spirit adds to our existent human nature, a union with the divine nature. We become partakers of the divine nature.

This aspect of the mystic union offers a twofold type.

The birth of Jesus by the Spirit is a type of *our* new birth (see John 3:7), and that is the initial work of the Spirit. We must all commence there. Then the birth of Jesus by the Spirit is a type of our sanctification (see Gal. 4:19). Think of this deep truth the apostle expresses. Writing to those Galatians, he tells them that he travailed in birth till Christ was formed in them. What is the significance of the word he uses? Simply this: As Mary surrendered her body to God the Father through the Holy Spirit and said, "Be it unto me according to thy word" (Luke 1:38), so we are to surrender ourselves to the Father through the same Holy Spirit that He might form Jesus within us. This is why we sing: "O Jesus Christ, grow thou in me."

JUSTIFIED BY THE SPIRIT
1 Timothy 3:16

"God was manifest in the flesh."

There you have our last aspect in the incarnation of Christ. God the Father becomes visible in Jesus Christ. Then comes this phrase, "justified in the Spirit" or as another translates it, "vindicated in the Spirit" (RSV). To what part of Jesus' life does this refer? It seems to me we can take that phrase "justified" or "vindicated" by the Spirit and stretch it over the thirty-three years of our Lord's life—more particularly to those so-called thirty "silent" years.

After the legal marriage of Joseph and Mary, children came into the home. In the course of time, Jesus found Himself bound to those who were connected with Him more or less by human ties. Here is what we read concerning His life there at Nazareth as He lived out His life for thirty years: "Neither did his brethren believe in him" (John 7:5). At the early age of twelve, He had to instruct His own mother. She could not understand the significance of His divine vocation. As He grew up among others, He was a mystery to them. He lived there in His home and was misunderstood. They misconstrued His motives. But here is the one truth that brings great comfort to our heart: Although He was misunderstood by those near Him, through it all, He had the justification or vindication of the Spirit. The Holy Spirit could say "amen" to everything Jesus said, thought, and accomplished.

Let us strive after the same justification of the Spirit. Jesus did not try to justify Himself. He left His justification to the Holy Spirit. He was not concerned about His reputation. We read that Jesus made Himself of no reputation. (*Reputation* is what people think of us; *character* is what God thinks of us.) We can afford to be independent, regarding our reputation, if we know that our character is godly. For no matter how people may misunderstand us and misconstrue our motives, if we are true to the Lord and have His mind and will concerning all things, sooner or later the justification of the Holy Spirit will be ours.

ANOINTED BY THE SPIRIT

Matthew 3:16

At the direction of God the Father, the Holy Spirit came upon Jesus at His baptism in the form of a dove and remained upon Him. Our Lord lays hold of an Old Testament Scripture (see Is. 42:1) and relates it to Himself. "I will put my spirit upon him" (Matt. 12:18) and so here for the first time, the Holy Spirit visibly comes upon Jesus. He has left His heavenly home. He is thinking of His ministry of three and one-half years. And the Holy Ghost took thirty years to prepare Jesus for a ministry of three and one-half years. There He stands at Jordan fully available to do His Father's business, and the Spirit of God comes upon Him in dovelike form.

This aspect of the mystic union between Father, Son, and Holy Spirit was clearly presented to my heart many years ago in Scotland. I was out walking around in a country district, reading, as I walked along, one of the greatest books on the Holy Spirit I know. In that volume, *The Ministry of the Spirit* by Dr. A. J. Gordon, is a chapter which makes very clear that, although Jesus was born of the Spirit and although He enjoyed the presence of the Spirit all through those thirty years, He required this distinct anointing of the Spirit ere He went into His ministry.

That requirement came to me with remarkable force. I had been a preacher for years, and I knew the truth of the Spirit. But somehow that aspect had never crept into my mind. Dr. Gordon says that we dare not face our work for the Lord unless we know something of this experience. I stopped in the middle of the road. Definitely and simply, I said to the Lord, *Grant unto me this anointing with the Spirit, that my service might be more vital and fruitful.*

Do you know what it is to have the Holy Spirit coming upon you? He has been within from the time of your regeneration, and you have realized more or less His companionship throughout your Christian pilgrimage. But have you had a crisis, when the Holy Spirit came upon you in some unique fashion, and service thereafter was different?

LED BY THE SPIRIT

Matthew 4:1

"Then was Jesus led up of the Spirit into the wilderness to be tempted of the devil."

That seems somewhat strange. We would have thought that after the anointing with the Holy Spirit that He would go forth immediately into Galilee and exercise His miraculous ministry. But no, He went into the wilderness to be tempted of the devil.

I remember how this came to me, too, with wonderful comfort, at the time to which I have already referred. I went home rejoicing that day after having that blessed transaction with the Spirit of God on that country lane. I have to confess that I was guilty of self-exultation. I said to myself, *Now I have looked to God, and I believe He has anointed me in some way and that He is going to accomplish greater things through my ministry.* I visualized greater opportunities—crowds being brought together and touched by the Spirit of God, and men and women bowed down under His convicting work.

But I was led into one of the darkest seasons of my Christian experience. A bitter test and grievous disappointment came to me. I was tempted to doubt the validity of that experience on the country road. Then I read this: "Then was Jesus led up of the Spirit into the wilderness to be tempted of the devil" (Matt. 4:1) And I thanked God and took courage.

At the back of any deep spiritual experience in which we meet God in a new way, is this satanic antagonism. And if God meets with you, as I trust He may, and you feel you are brought up onto the mountain top—watch out! When you have been visited by the Spirit of God and vow that life is going to be altogether different insofar as you are concerned—take caution! Back in your routine, you will find yourself up against satanic activity. Remember this: Jesus went from Jordan with the Father's benediction from heaven into the wilderness for a battle with the Devil. Perhaps you know that this word "led" occurs twice in our Lord's ministry—at the beginning of it and at the end of it. "Then was Jesus *led* up of the Spirit" (Matt. 4:1, italics added). "They . . . *led* him away to crucify him" (Matt. 27:31, italics added). And there is always a Cross for a Spirit-led believer.

EMPOWERED BY THE SPIRIT
Luke 4:14–18

"And Jesus returned in the power of the Spirit into Galilee: and there went out a fame of Him through all the region." (Luke 4:14).

But Galilee came after the wilderness experience. Note the order: Jordan, the wilderness, then Galilee. You can never be of great use out in *your* Galilee until you know something of *your* wilderness. You can never lead men and women above the level of your own experience. And unless you know what it is to meet the full weight and strength of the foe as Jesus did in the wilderness, you can never be the means of victory to those who are defeated around you.

What happened then? He had power over Satan—power over sin and power over sickness. He healed multitudes without medicine and made no charge for His service. Power was manifested in the Person of the Spirit. Sometimes we hear believers in prayer meetings pleading with God to give them power, as if power is a mysterious something He empties out upon them. The power is a person. Jesus said: "Ye shall receive power, after that the Holy Ghost is come upon you" (Acts 1:8).

So the Holy Spirit working through our Lord made possible His miraculous ministry.

GLADDENED BY THE SPIRIT

Luke 10:21

In the Revised Standard Version, this text reads, "he rejoiced in the Holy Spirit." Dr. Weymouth translates it as follows: "And Jesus Christ was filled with rapturous joy through the Holy Spirit." We carry with us a false conception of our Lord, perhaps inspired by artists who always give us somber portraits of the face of Jesus. It is perfectly true that Jesus was the Man of sorrows and acquainted with grief. But let us never forget that it is recorded of Him that He was anointed with the oil of gladness above His fellows. He was the happiest Man of His day.

Here you have the source of His joy—the Holy Ghost. In Romans 14:17 the apostle Paul brings the Holy Spirit and joy together, when he speaks about "joy in the Holy Ghost." You remember that on the day of Pentecost, those disciples became God-intoxicated people. Because of their elation, the people said: "These men are full of new wine" (Acts 2:13). But they were filled with joy and the Holy Ghost.

Then the fruit of the Spirit includes joy (see Gal. 5:22). We need to know something of this in our Christian work, do we not? There is much to disappoint and to depress us. If we are not careful, we give way to our feelings. We need to know something of the Holy Spirit as the source of joy.

There is a difference between happiness and joy. Dr. Griffith Thomas was very fond of explaining the difference. He said that happiness depends upon what happens. If things do not happen, then we are not very happy. But joy is independent of all circumstances. We have an illustration of that in Acts 16. There are Paul and his companion sitting on the floor in that dark dungeon, their backs lashed and the blood oozing forth. Yet at midnight you find them singing praises to God. There was joy, and the Holy Ghost was the source of the apostle's joy. We also find joy in the Holy Ghost.

In a good many evangelistic circles today, jazz and rock are being mistaken for joy. I have been in a few of these circles where emotions are played upon and things are worked up to such a pitch, people believe they are having a happy time. But the whole thing is temporary. An hour after the meeting, the feeling has evaporated. What we need, beloved, in our own inner life and in our service, is the continuing joy the Holy Ghost makes possible.

SUSTAINED IN DEATH BY THE SPIRIT
Hebrews 9:14, Acts 5:32

The Holy Spirit, who together with the Father made possible the humanity of Jesus and accompanied Him all through His testing, was present all through the ministry of our Lord. The Spirit upheld and sustained Him as He was stretched out upon a wooden cross.

Did you ever think of this: In the persons of God the Father and of the Holy Spirit we have the only living witnesses in the universe today to the sufferings of Jesus? Peter described the agonies of Jesus: "We are his witnesses of these things [the agonies of Jesus]; and so is also the Holy Ghost" (Acts 5:32). The first chain of eyewitnesses passed away 1900 years ago, but we still have the remaining witnesses—God the Father and God the Holy Spirit.

That is of great encouragement to me as a preacher for this reason: When I stand before unconverted men and and women and preach the Cross, relying upon the Holy Ghost, I know that the message will be blessed. He can project the image of the Cross to the unconverted. He made it possible. That is how the preaching of the Cross is the power of God unto salvation.

Spiritually, we can die in the same way. In Romans 8 Paul speaks of mortifying the deeds of the body. How can we die spiritually? Only by the Spirit! The Father and the Holy Spirit had been with Jesus all through the thirty-three earthly years until His body was stretched out on the cross. I like to think the Holy Spirit was in the tomb guarding that body of Jesus.

The Roman government set its seal on the outside of the tomb, indicating that Jesus would not rise. God the Father had His seal inside, declaring that Jesus would rise again. The Holy Ghost is our seal (see Eph. 4:30). I love to think of God's sending the Holy Spirit to guard the body of Jesus, for through the Spirit He made possible the resurrection of Christ.

RAISED BY THE SPIRIT
Romans 8:11

"The Spirit of him that raised up Jesus from the dead."

He was responsible for His glorified body. As the Spirit of life, He is responsible for resurrection. Because we are under the Father's care and are indwelt by the same Holy Spirit, we know that one day we shall share in the resurrection of our Lord. We, too, after death, will be "quickened [made alive] by the Spirit" (1 Pet. 3:18).

COMMANDED BY THE SPIRIT

Acts 1:2

I do not know whether you have come up against the odd teaching that the "church" is not an important New Testament doctrine. Some claim we find the church nowhere in the Acts, that all we have in the New Testament about the church is three Epistles, and that Pentecost is not the birthday of the church.

I beg to differ. I believe Pentecost is the birthday of the church and that the Book of Acts contains the establishment of the church of God. Then, as you journey on, you have its extension. Here is a word that convinces me of this truth: "He through the Holy Ghost had given commandments unto the apostles" (Acts 1:2). What do you find in the Acts? The apostles went out and, through their ministry, churches were established. What our Lord gave them that day by the Holy Ghost became the polity of the churches they established.

You can prove that by turning to 1 Thessalonians 4:2: "Ye know what commandments we gave you by the Lord Jesus." No matter where you turn in the Acts of the Apostles, you have development of the truth that Jesus gave that day to His apostles by the Holy Spirit. You dare not face a Sunday school class, a sinner friend, or a congregation, in an attempt to transmit to them any truth, without being conscious of being inspired by the same Spirit.

PROVIDED OUR MODEL BY THE SPIRIT

1 John 2:6

"He that saith he abideth in him [Jesus] ought himself also so to walk, even as he walked."

How did Jesus walk? He walked in the Spirit, relying

upon His Father. Are we allowing all our thoughts, words, feelings, actions, pleasures, and pursuits to be saturated through and through with the Holy Spirit? Our Lord was full of the Spirit, and if He who was divine had need of the ministry of the Spirit, how deep is our need?

Let us believe and claim the promise of Acts 1:8, "Ye shall receive power, after that the Holy Ghost is come upon you: and ye shall be witnesses unto me both in Jerusalem, and in all Judaea, and in Samaria, and unto the uttermost part of the earth." Let us forsake all known sin, for He is the Spirit of Holiness. We cannot undertake great service if there is anything contrary to His holy mind and will.

Then let us respond immediately to the faintest whisper of His voice. In your Christian life and service and as you come up against the problems of the world, remember that doubt regarding the rightness of certain behavior can be taken as the voice of the Spirit. If we give the Holy Spirit the benefit of the doubt, we find ourselves victorious.

The victorious Christian life depends upon a close relation to the Trinity. "The grace of the Lord Jesus Christ, and the love of God, and the communion of the Holy Ghost, be with you all. Amen" (2 Cor. 13:14).

6

Christ—Root and Star

"I am the root . . . and the . . . star" (Rev. 22:16).

Life is, at its best, incomplete and fragmentary. Christ, however, combines the most opposing temperaments and reconciles the diversities of our being. He can do this, seeing that He is not only a man but Man. Everything that *all* men were meant to be, our Savior actually was and *is*. In a sinless manhood, He embraced all the noble traits of the human race. Varying, yet perfect, ideals were blended in a perfect unity within the perfect character of Jesus.

Note the union of apparent contradictions and the meeting of extremes in the person and work of our adorable Lord. Qualities of a diverse character are brought into complete harmony in Him.

His glory is seen in the combination He exhibited of gentleness and firmness. He was somewhat like the eagle, known as the "king of birds." It has not only a stern eye, firm beak, and strong talons, which enable it to grip the rock, but a soft, downy breast where the eaglets can nestle for warmth and comfort and safety. Thus is it with Christ. He has kingly majesty and gentle grace. He is strong, yet sympathetic. He is lordly, yet loving. What else can we do but love Him, whose countenance is majesty, whose life is love, whose hand is omnipotence, whose eye is bountifulness, whose heart is compassion, and whose smile is heaven? Truly, He is great and greatly to be praised! And such a harmony of opposites suggests two observations.

1. Jesus was not one-sided. His character contained no narrow limits of individuality that usually beset the great of earth. When we think of Napoleon, we think of a warrior; of Columbus, of a discoverer; of Abraham Lincoln, of an emancipator; of Paul, of a theologian; of John, a beloved disciple. Those who are most gifted usually stress the one-sidedness of their qualities.

Jesus, however, does not draw some and drive others away because of any oddities, or peculiarities, such as a genius often has. Our Lord has no idiosyncracies. He was perfectly whole, emotionally symmetrical, combining with a remarkable equality all the traits of human life. Therefore, He is adapted to all. He is the Garment that fits each body, yet is owned and dominated by no one, seeing that He is distinct from all others.

2. Jesus could reconcile opposite offices and functions within His person. He is the Shepherd and the Lamb; the Priest and the Sacrifice; the Vine and the Branch; the King and the Servant. He, Himself, tells us that He is the Root and the Bright and Morning Star.

Consider the world of difference between a root and a star. There is no natural unity existent between the two; they are utterly unlike. Yet Christ unites both objects in His own Being. Taken separately, the figures are rich in spiritual significance. Taken together, they bring encouragement to our hearts. For having diversity in Himself, such as roots and stars suggest, we can find all we need in Him who is both the "Root" and the "Star." Let us now seek to trace the teaching underlining this double metaphor.

LOCAL YET UNIVERSAL

The root is local, embedded in a single spot. It grows from a seed in certain soil and must stay where it finds nourishment. The star, on the other hand, is universal; shedding its light and influence upon the world. Whether persons pause in a crowded city, in a lonely glen, or amid the solitude of an ocean, they can lift up their eyes to heaven and be comforted by the shining star.

Roots, then, grow in one place and have a fixed, definite locality. Stars, on the other hand, are the joy of all localities. Their brilliance is for the world. Thus is it with Christ, our Lord. Born in Bethlehem, He grew up in Nazareth. In the days of His flesh, He never traveled beyond the Holy Land. Yet today He is the Light of the World. The root out of a dry ground has now a universal radiance. Go to dark Africa, and you will find Him there. The frozen North and India's coral strand alike hold His followers. Although rooted in the rich soil of Palestine in the days of His flesh as David's Son and Lord, admired only by a few, He now shines, with a light serene—the Bright and Morning Star!

Although He came of Jewish stock, He is not limited by the narrow bounds of nationality. He is a Jew always and everywhere. But all nations claim Christ, seeing that He is "the desire of all nations" (Hag. 2:7). A solution for racial problems, then, is the presentation of Christ in His fullness. And once an ethnic group receives Him, it sees Jesus through its own culture's eyes.

And a further feature of the gospel is that I can make Him my very own personal Savior and Lord—independent of the color of my skin and the peculiarities of my personality.

SECRET YET REVEALED

Looking again at the apocalyptic figures, we can discern a union between the secret and the seen, the hidden and the revealed.

A root is an object concealed from observation. Whether just under the surface or deep in the earth, roots shun the light and have their sustenance in the darkness.

A star, however, is for all to see. On the brightest day, no one can see a buried root; but on the darkest night, the evening star ever twinkles.

Christ is unique in that He combines the known and the unknown. "The darkness and the light are both alike to thee" (Ps. 139:12). As a Root, He is hidden in glory and buried in our heart. Yet He cannot be hid. If He is hidden in your devotional life as a Root, then through your relationships He will shine as a Star, revealing in some way or other the radiance of His presence.

Further, Christ is known, yet unknown. While there is much that we can see of His glory and majesty, and much we can understand of His grace and power, He is beyond human comprehension. There are mysteries in Him a person will never fathom, aspects of His character beyond human ken. We can walk in His light as the Star, yet never penetrate the roots of His Deity, wisdom, and fullness.

EARTHLY YET HEAVENLY

Roots and stars, belonging as they do to different worlds, suggest that Jesus is a citizen of both worlds.

A root is a common child of earth where the feet of toilers tread, lovers walk, and children play. The root is the part of a plant fastened to earth.

A star, on the other hand, has its dwelling in the solitary heights of heaven. It is beyond all human reach. It is conspicuous among the glories of the sky.

Extreme locations meet in Christ. As the Root and Offspring of David, He came from the royal house. He was the "root of Jesse" (Is. 11:10); the "Root of David" (Rev. 5:5). Human descent and true humanity were His. He had a human mother, required a baby's clothing and care, toiled, suffered, and wept as a Man. Like the Tribe of Judah from which He sprang, He took "root downward" (2 Kings 19:30). And yet amid His earthly life, He manifested the shining, lofty brilliance of Deity. Although from heaven, He ever remained "in heaven" (John 3:13), showing a timeless existence for the omnipresent Son. He was not too heavenly to be of earthly use; nor too earthly to be of heavenly use. He balanced both worlds in His one person.

And such a combination brings hope and comfort to our hearts, seeing that we need the continual assistance of this heavenly, earthly Friend. We are all like roots. The majority of us have to live out our days in some fixed spot. Some are planted, grow, die, and are buried within the same locality. Days are filled up with common duties and ministries of earth. Life develops, like a root, amid things of earth.

Yet the glory of the commonplace can be ours. Our spirits can shine as stars; we can live in the heavenlies. A radiance not of earth can surround our life and path.

Some are all root—of the earth, earthy. Others are all stars—they live in the clouds. Harmony, however, must reign between roots and stars.

We can find Him in both situations of our lives. Buried amid things of earth, we have by our side the Root and Offspring of David. As the Man Christ Jesus, He is touched with the feeling of our infirmity. But as the Bright and Morning Star He seeks to fill our common, ordinary life with light supernatural. May He enable us to have more starry brilliance about our lives, counteracting thereby much of the earth clinging to us as roots!

HUMAN YET DIVINE

A further application of the opposite metaphors we are considering brings us to the truth of our Lord's dual nature.

A root is planted by the hand of man, is earth-grown, and develops under the care of the gardener. Though created by God, roots are nurtured by human beings.

A star is of a different order. It is planted in the heavens by the hand divine. Though observed by humanity, stars are created by God.

In Christ, Deity and humanity are united into the perfect whole. He was God in the flesh. In His condescension, He became the Root and Offspring of David. He commenced His human years in a cradle of straw and ended it in a well-spiced grave. The human, historic Jesus really existed. Some there were who knew Him only after the flesh. To them He was never more than a Root.

But Jesus was God's Son, not just Mary's Child; the mighty God as well as the Babe wrapped in swaddling clothes; the Star of heaven as well as the Root of earth.

The star by which the wise men were guided was the symbol of the starry Deity of Him who was born a Babe. To most religious leaders, Jesus was only another Jew; but to the Spirit-anointed eyes of Peter, He was the Christ, the Son of the living God.

TEMPORARY YET ABIDING

Both transient and eternal qualities will be evident when you study these two figures of speech Jesus employs to describe Himself.

A root is a temporary thing. It begins with a seed. The seed is sown and gradually sends out its tiny roots to grow amid the darkness of the soil. The root serves its purpose and then perishes and dies (see Job 14:8).

A star is different. Stars abide. The stars which shone upon Adam and Eve amid the beauties of Eden have continued to shine upon the millions inhabiting the world ever since. Stars never change. Astronomers have opened for us the starry heavens through the use of powerful telescopes and space observatories. It seems the universe is ever expanding.

Roots, then, come and go, but the stars go on forever. Roots are temporary; stars, permanent and perpetual. Thus is it with Christ. As the Root, He had a temporary manifestation, remaining only some thirty-three years. He came, lived His life, and crossed the stage of time. Then the place that knew Him ceased to know Him as the Man of Nazareth. But when people buried Him as the Root, He did not decay. He arose, and is alive as God and Man forevermore. And I believe that soon all the redeemed will behold His returning, as the Bright and Morning Star.

JEWISH YET CHRISTIAN

It would seem as if the two metaphors before us express the twofold relationship that is highlighted in the Book of the Revelation.

As the Root and Offspring of David there is the assertion of Christ's connection with Israel in royalty. He came as the King of the Jews, but was rejected as David's Lord and Heir. Yet, He will be seen as the promised Messiah, the King of Israel. When He returns to earth with Israel looking upon Him who was pierced, He will serve the nations of the world once more as the long-diverted channel of divine grace.

As the Bright and Morning Star, Jesus is associated with His church. Before the Tribulation and Millennium eras, He will appear as the Star to His Bride. As the Sun of Righteousness He will arise upon Israel with noonday splendor. But as the morning star appears long before the midday sun, so Jesus will first appear as the Morning Star for His redeemed. The Morning Star is the harbinger of day. Now, from the heights, He watches His church toiling against contrary winds. But before long, on some particular day, He will come again to take His own to the eternal land of light and love.

Until the Bright and Morning Star bursts upon the darkness of the world, let us hitch the little wagons of our lives to Him who is the hidden Star. Then, although we live out our lives as roots of earth, we will yet shine. I know this fact because God's Word assures me of it. I want you to have that same assurance and hope. Meditate on this beautiful promise: "They that be wise shall shine as the brightness of the firmament; and they that turn many to righteousness as the stars for ever and ever" (Dan. 12:3).

7

The Lion and the Lamb

Within the Apocalypse, John, the inspired apostle, records a strange spectacle of suspense in the heavenly courts. "Behold, the Lion . . . . and I beheld, and, lo, in the midst of the throne . . . stood a Lamb" (Rev. 5:5–6).

Recall the setting. The seven-sealed book was in the palm of the Eternal One, but wonder abounded on every side, for none was found worthy to open and read the scroll. Such failure caused John to weep. An elder, however, bade John not to grieve but to turn and behold a prevailing Lion. But looking, as directed, John saw not a Lion in his majesty, but a Lamb (or a little Lamb, as the original really implies).

During one of the sport days in the ancient Roman Colosseum, the crowds sat watching as a martyr stood in the arena waiting for a lion to leap forth from its cage. The cry had rent the air: "The Christians to the lions!" Suddenly, however, as a diversion for the Roman crowds, the keeper led forth a gentle lamb instead of a semi-starved lion. The gentle animal stepped forward and licked the hand of the martyr amid the surprise and thunderous applause of the crowded amphitheatre. One animal symbolized peace; the other, destruction. John turned to behold the Lord Jesus Christ at the center of glory as a Lion but saw Him as a Lamb. And there is no contradiction between the two metaphors. One of the elders cried, "Behold, the Lion" (Rev. 5:5), but John, from the earth side, answers, "Behold, a Lamb" (see Rev. 5:6). And their voices echo the need of both descriptions to show forth the fullness of His glory.

The Lion and the Lamb are two figures of speech which indicate a double truth we must be careful never to separate in the work of salvation within the human soul. Christ is needed not only as the Lamb to expiate the guilt of sin but as the Lion to conquer the power of sin. As the Lamb, He wins back a lost inheritance for us. As the Lion, He unfolds the inheritance, making it actual in our lives. As the Lamb He saves and redeems; as the Lion He holds sway and rules.

The sealed roll or book to which John refers can be looked upon as the title deed of man's heavenly inheritance, lost by the fall in Eden but won back for the sinner by the Lamb of God at Calvary. The book, however, is sealed. Its contents are unavailable until someone with authority and power is able to break the seals. And it is here that Christ's double role is necessary. He is not only the Lamb of atoning sacrifice but the Lion of majestic royal conquest. By priestly self-sacrifice, Jesus opened up the way to eternal life. Vested with kingly power, He can make believers victorious over sinful habits and tastes which hinder the experience and enjoyment of His finished work. As the Lamb, Christ can save; as the Lion, He can keep us saved.

Here we have extremes in the animal world. The lion is majestic; the lamb, the meekest of animals. One is strong; the other, weak. One is fearless; the other, fearful. Yet there is no contradiction whatever when both figures are applied to Christ, who, as we shall see, combined both in His life and labor.

Isaiah, in describing the millennial reign of the Messiah, tells us that "the wolf also shall dwell with the lamb" (11:6). I understand that Jehovah's Witnesses believe we are now in the Millennium. The fallacy of such an assertion can be proved by placing a lamb alongside a wolf or a lion. Certainly they could dwell together today, but it would be with the lamb *inside* the lion and not alongside him.

In Christ, however, the Lion and the Lamb are in complete blissful harmony. Both dignity and lowliness of bearing are ever evident. Our Lord combined the brave, courageous attitude of a nobleman and the gentle ministering touch of a woman. Having a royal bearing, He could yet stoop to serve as a slave.

Both mastery and suffering made up His career. Both self-assertion and self-sacrifice characterized His earthly sojourn.

Authority and entreaty are everywhere in His dealings. The voice that casts out demons also pleads with the demon-possessed to come and rest. Eyes that flash with wrath as they look at hypocrites also melt with compassion over a doomed city.

Thus, all through the gospel story, we can detect this double strain. Everywhere there is the mysterious blending of Deity and humanity. The Lion and the Lamb are together. Christ is lionlike in His passion of hate over all forces that rob humanity of peace and blessedness. Christ is lamblike in His tenderness and compassion for the robbed sinner. The lionlike majesty is seen in His rebuke of the wind and waves; His lamblike meekness, in that, being reviled, He reviled not again.

His lionlike power was manifested at the grave of Lazarus as He shouted, "Lazarus, come forth" (John 11:43). His lamblike patience is evident when before Herod He opened not His mouth (see Luke 23:7–9). The lionlike boldness is seen in His setting of His face steadfastly toward Jerusalem; the lamblike grace comes out in His unwillingness to strive or cry.

His lionlike sternness can be detected in His condemnation of Jerusalem that "killest the prophets, and stonest them which are sent unto thee" (Matt. 23:37). His lamblike tenderness drips with His tears over Jerusalem.

His lionlike assertiveness emerges in the Gospel of John's succession of "I ams"; His lamblike self-denial emerges in that, although He was the Light, He endured darkness. As the Bread of Life, He hungered. As the King, He suffered as a slave. As the Lord of Life, He died.

His lionlike loftiness as He claims the allegiance of man can be traced in His declaration, "He that loveth father or mother more than me is not worthy of me" (Matt. 10:37). His lamblike depth of sacrifice for men is suggested by His willingness to make Himself of no reputation.

Paul speaks of the goodness and severity of the Lord, and the two figures before us express these two qualities.

John gives us a summary of the Revelation in the twofold vision of Christ as Lamb and King. "The Lamb shall overcome them: for He is Lord of lords, and King of kings" (Rev. 17:14). As the Chief and King of men and women, Jesus must be foremost in suffering. Christ, because He is Savior, must endure grief. As the Captain of our salvation, He must be made perfect through suffering. Suffering perfects character, and it increases sympathy and power.

A very interesting legend is recorded of a chasm in the center of the Roman Forum, caused by the people incurring the wrath of the gods. The rift grew wider and wider day by day. Citizens poured all their richest possessions—gold, silver, and jewels—into the gulf, but it yawned wider and more terrible. It was decided that the only way to close it was Rome's noblest citizen's casting himself in. Curtius, one of the noblest of youths, leapt in astride his snow-white horse. The abyss closed. Curtius, a lion of Rome, had to become a lamb of expiation.

Thus was it with Christ. By His incarnation, He became the Chief of Men, the Noblest of All, imposing upon Himself thereby the work of atonement. "It was expedient that one man should die for the people" (John 18:14). Bethlehem necessitated Calvary. The Virgin Birth and the Vicarious Death go together. Because Christ was the Lion, He alone could become the Lamb.

The strong, immortal Son of God, so perfect and holy, is presented as the Lion of God, and as such has the right to die as the Lamb of God for our sins. The prevailing Lion became the prevailing Lamb. Only God manifest in the flesh can cause all flesh to be saved.

Another way of dealing with these two descriptive metaphors is to apply them to Christ's double work. He became the Lion in His resurrection, because He was willing to die as the Lamb at Calvary. And He is ever lionized as the Lamb in Heaven. "Worthy is the Lamb . . . to receive power, and riches, and wisdom, and strength, and honour, and glory, and blessing" (Rev. 5:12).

> Crown Him with many crowns
> The Lamb upon His Throne.

Lionlike, He "shall divide the spoil with the strong," because lamblike, He "hath poured out His soul unto death" (Is. 53:12). As the Lamb, He goes to slaughter; as the Lion, He leads to victory. As the Lamb, He is rejected; as the Lion, He reigns. His crown is reached by way of the Cross. Suffering led to sovereignty; humiliation, to honor. Christ reigns from the tree.

A greater, more startling contrast could scarcely be conceived than that existing between a lion and a lamb. John expects to see a Lion, and beholds a Lamb. So we have the Christ of Jewish expectation, and the Christ of reality. What kind of Messiah did the Jews expect? Did they not look for a conquering prince who would deliver them from their foes and restore the kingdom (see Acts 1:6)? But how disappointed they were! Instead of a King in royal robe and a retinue of servants, He came as the despised One. He was born, not in a palace, but a stable. Instead of a Lion fighting Israel's foes, He allowed Himself to be led as a Lamb, silently and submissively, to slaughter.

This is still the conception of Him held by the world. The multitudes clamor for power and force. They have little room for tenderness, gentleness, sacrifice, and love. Dictators preach the survival of the fittest. The world's way of achieving power is by war. Modern history provides plenty of room for lions but none for lambs. God's method of conquest, however, is by sacrifice. Over against the clenched fist is the nail-pierced hand of Christ. And let it never be forgotten that that pierced hand will yet wield the scepter of universal dominion.

Our meditation on the Lion and the Lamb suggests a twofold application:

1. Accept His lionlike qualities. We need Christ in the twofold office as Lion and Lamb, fulfilled in and through us. Do we know Him as both? We know Him as the Lamb slain for us. We have accepted Him as the sole ground of our acceptance before God. But is He the Lion

ruling over us? Have we surrendered all to Him as the prevailing One? As the Lamb, He has delivered us from the penalty of our past sins. But as the Lion, is He emancipating us from the power and thralldom of sin as day follows day? If saved by the blood of the Lamb, we must fight under His leadership against the other lion that Peter calls "a roaring lion . . . seeking whom he may devour" (1 Pet. 5:8).

2. Develop both qualities. As Christ's followers, we must let a twofold spirit characterize our lives. We must be "kings and priests unto God" (Rev. 1:6). Lionlike power, strength, and courage and lamblike meekness, gentleness, and submission should form our dual nature. Some Christians have too much of one side and not enough of the other. Only He who is the Lion *and* the Lamb can give us the balance between the two.

As lambs we must be meek under injury, patient amid suffering, submissive to God, self-sacrificial on behalf of others, always as sheep amid wolves.

As lions we must exhibit boldness against all evil forces and be active and aggressive in doing God's work. How we need more of the lionlike character in these apostate days! Many of us are too passive. We do not try to win against evil, seeing we do not expect to reign in the Christian life. Yet we are always more than conquerors when sheltered by the blood of the Lamb and mantled with the power of the Lion.

8

An Abundance of Good Names

"What can we name the baby?" This question worries many expectant parents. They consider names that sound good or belong to some well-known person.

For myself, three surnames were given me as the first child of my parents:

> Herbert, my father's name
> Henry, my grandfather's name
> John, my uncle's name.

But with the wondrous birth of God's beloved Son, it was otherwise. There was no worry about or searching for a name. His glorious names were not left to human choice. Thus, He is worshiped by and understood by His names divine.

The titles given to the Savior in the two birth narratives express the wonder of the Child who was born that He might die for our salvation. Let us gather these titles together. Reverently consider these names, that at any season, our hearts may magnify the Christ who made

Christmas possible and love Him who was born as the Babe of Bethlehem.

Although we may be able to explain the significance of the names given to Mary's Holy Child, the human mind could never unfold the overwhelming mystery of the Incarnation. Our Lord's names, however, help us to comprehend His many qualities; like the ointment of the Tabernacle, compounded of several spices, His names are varied.

JESUS
"Thou shalt call his name JESUS" (Matt. 1:21).

This name is used in the opening verse of the New Testament (see Matt. 1:1); likewise in the final verse (see Rev. 22:21). The benediction, closing the Book of Revelation, contains our Lord's triad of outstanding designations, "our Lord Jesus Christ."

"Jesus," a common Jewish name at the time of Christ's birth, stands out as the title of His humanity and humiliation. It means "Jehovah, the Savior", and it is, therefore, His human name, connecting Him with the work of salvation. This fact is made clear in the message of the angel of the Lord to Joseph: "Thou shalt call his name JESUS: for he shall save his people from their sins" (Matt. 1:21).

Note that He has power to save "his people from their sins." Thus He is the Savior of saints as well as of sinners. His people have a good many sins to be saved from, and it is encouraging to know that He is "the Savior of all men, specially of those that believe" (1 Tim. 4:10). Yes, and no other name has endeared Him to our heart and is enshrined in so many Christ-honoring hymns as this one by which Mary called her Child.

CHRIST

"Jesus who is called Christ" (Matt. 27;22, RSV).

From *Christos*, meaning *Anointed*, we have in this designation our Lord's official name. This name connects Him with the Old Testament dispensation, seeing that he came as the fulfiller of prophecy. As an Old Testament term, the name before us was applied to those anointed with holy oil. At His baptism, Jesus was anointed for His threefold office of prophet, priest, and king and officially became the Christ.

Later on, the apostles used *Christ* as the name of a changed position, seeing that He had been raised from the dead and exalted in glory. Yes,

Christ is a Prophet, Priest, and King;
   A Prophet full of light,
A Priest that stands 'twixt God and man,
   A King that rules with might.
My Christ, He is the Heaven of heavens;
   My Christ, what shall I call?
My Christ is first, my Christ is last;
   My Christ is all in all.

It will be remembered that Peter received a divine revelation in order to assert: "Thou art the Christ, the Son of the living God" (Matt. 16:16). This blessed name is associated also with the believer, for he is known as a "Christian", that is, a follower of the Anointed One. May the Holy Spirit make us more Christlike.

LORD

"A Savior, which is Christ the Lord" (Luke 2:11).

This title indicates authority and dominion. Though He was despised as Jesus, the world will yet see Him as the Lord of Lords. To those of us who know and love Him, He is Lord and God even now, as we linger in a world so hostile to His claims. More than ever may we sanctify Him as Lord in our hearts!

There is, however, a beautiful combination in the angelic message. Like a prism, it flashes out many rich colors. When our Lord is referred to as "Jesus Christ," the emphasis is upon Jesus, the humble humiliated One, now glorified. But when the designation is reversed, then as "Christ Jesus" you see Him as the despised One, now glorified. His full and rightful title, "The Lord Jesus Christ," suggests added authority and power: "God hath made that same Jesus, . . . both Lord and Christ" (Acts 2:36).

As a "Savior", He is able to deliver from all evil and to endow the delivered with all good. It is essential to note that He was *born* a Savior.

EMMANUEL

"They shall call his name Emmanuel, which being interpreted is, God with us" (Matt. 1:23).

This precious name reveals the further and fuller purpose of God. In His goodness, He delights to tabernacle among men. In the Old Testament, He has a tabernacle for His people—now He has His people as a tabernacle. In fact, Scripture can be generally summarized thus: In the Old Testament, it is God *for* us; in the Gospels, God *with* us; in the Epistles, God *in* us. The latter, being the ideal, contains all that the first two aspects promise.

"Emmanuel!" Truly this is a revelation of His character we can cling to in the dark and difficult hours of life. Because He has promised never to leave us, we can count upon His abiding companionship.

As God, He came from heaven, bringing God to man.

As the glorified Man, He went back from earth to heaven, reconciling man to God. In Him the chasm is bridged between the Creator and the creature—between a thrice holy God and the lost sinner.

> "God with us" in the world of sin,
>   This life of weakness and of woe:
> His love, His power and His strength
>   With us, wherever we may go.
> Since Jesus came to earth to dwell
> And be for aye, Emmanuel.
>
> No weary days, no starless nights,
>   No sorrow deep, no trials sore,
> But we can feel His presence near,
>   "God with us" now and evermore,
> Since He hath come to earth to dwell
> Whose name is still Emmanuel.

KING

"Where is he that is born King of the Jews?" (Matt. 2:2).

What a striking phrase this is in the question of the wise men! "Born King!" No one of royal blood is born a king. A prince becomes a king upon the death of his father. But Jesus was *born* a King, implying that He was a King before He was born. The Babe of Bethlehem was "the King eternal" (1 Tim. 1:17).

Christ was a truer King than Herod, who sought the young Child's life. Herod was known as a murderer; Jesus, as the Giver of life. Herod received his throne from Rome; Jesus, from heaven. Indeed Jesus is the King of kings.

Strange insignia of royalty, however, awaited the King. His palace was a stable; His throne, a mother's knee; His courtiers, the lowly shepherds; His robe, the swaddling clothes. Truly, He was a King in disguise. May we be found among the number who recognize and revere Him as King of the saints and who yield unto Him the undivided sway He deserves and demands! The valiant knight said of Arthur, "We never saw his like; there lives no greater leader." But the glory of King Arthur pales into nothingness alongside of the richer glory of Christ our King. It is thus we sing: "Hail Jesus, King of my days and nights!"

GOVERNOR

"Out of thee shall come a Governor, that shall rule" (Matt. 2:6).

While all the names before us are more or less associated with the Jews, they hold a larger application. Here for example, as Governor, Jesus is to have power to rule His people Israel. But of the increase of His government there is to be no end (see Is. 9:7). The word used in Matthew 2:6 for *Governor* means, "one who goes first, leads the way, chief in war." Jesus has every right to lead the way, seeing that He triumphed gloriously in His war against sin and Satan.

Yes, and as a Governor, He is not a hard despot. He rules by love. The word, *rule*, in Matthew 2:6, means *to shepherd*. Jesus protects and feeds. Some governors who rise from the ranks become unsympathetic and officious; not so the Lord Jesus, even though He was our fellow. He attracts us to follow Him by His scars, not His sword. His sufferings give Him sovereignty. Triumph is His because he bore a cross.

If we would govern in life, we must be cross-bearers, for the death of self ever leads to a diadem. We triumph in life when we "lay in dust life's glory, dead."

The prophet Isaiah would have us remember that of the increase of Christ's government there is to be no end. Universal dominion is to be His. There are to be no disputed borders to His kingdom.

But, can it be said that His government is increasing spiritually and personally? As He claims more territory, are we prepared to tear down the barriers and let Him take possession? If we do, we can expect Satan to contest every inch of ground we yield to the all-conquering Christ.

SON

"Son of David" (Matt. 1:1).

Kingship and royalty are prominent in this designation. Jesus was of the Davidic line and was born in the City of David. And, coming of the house and lineage of David, He was, as the Son of David, the Successor of David and Heir of all the promises granted to him (see Luke 1:32, 2:4).

"Son of Abraham" (Matt. 1:1).

Covenant relationship is here in view. At His wondrous birth, Jesus' relationship as the seed of Abraham was evident. Jesus was a Hebrew, descended from the father of His race.

"Her firstborn son" (Matt. 1:25).

Nine times over, Jesus is referred to as "the young child." Son of a woman, He was, but never the Son of a man. As Mary's Child, our Lord possessed actual humanity. That He never forgot this relationship is seen in His tender solicitude concerning her future, as He said when He was about to die: "Behold thy son!" (John 19:26). Committing Mary to John's care, He bade His favorite disciple treat her as a mother.

"Out of Egypt have I called my son" (Matt. 2:15).

As Mary's Child, Christ was born. As God's Son, He was given. Deity is wrapped up in this filial term. And what sublime contrasts are associated with the Virgin Birth! He was the Son, yet the Lord of heaven; the Babe, yet the Ancient of Days; Jesus, the Son of Man, yet Christ the Mighty God.

We can link to this designation the kindred one of "Son of the Highest" (Luke 1:32), which is a theocratic title pointing to Him as the Anointed (see Ps. 2:7; 89:27). Incidentally, we have a most helpful combination of terms in Luke's birth narrative. Notice these four examples: Jesus is the Son of the Highest; God the Father is in the Highest; the Holy Spirit is the Power of the Highest; and John the Baptist is the Prophet of the Highest (see Luke 1:32; 2:14; 1:35, 76).

"My Son"! What does this mean? It expresses divine filial relationship, imposing the obligation of separation. The remarkable thing is that God condescends to call *us* His sons: "Ye are sons" (Gal. 4:6). What a privilege! But, hasn't He called us out of Egypt, typical as it is of the world and bondage? Yes! What unworthy children we are if we hanker after the fleshpots of Egypt! If the world has claimed us, we can only be truly happy if we come completely out of such a spiritual Egypt.

NAZARENE

"He shall be called a Nazarene" (Matt. 2:23).

To be called a Nazarene was to be declared despicable. It was equivalent to shame and contempt. The town was not mentioned in the Old Testament. "Can there any good thing come out of Nazareth?" (John 1:46) was the significant query of one who knew that town.

When Christ's mangled form was stretched out upon the cross, His name was written above Him—"JESUS OF NAZARETH" (John 19:19). And a true Nazarene He was, for did He not stoop to the lowest depths of ignominy on our behalf? For our salvation He was willing to endure hatred, contempt, and all that was despicable. For Christ's followers, true commitment means the willingness to go outside the camp, bearing His reproach. As they hold aloof from the useless frivolities of a fun-craving culture, they know what it is to be treated with contempt. The truer a Christian is to the Nazarene, the once-despised Jesus, the more intense is the ill will, hatred, and rejection by worldly minded friends. Nazareth, however, has lost its negative reputation through Christ's contact with the place. The town is a type, surely, of grace, seeing that He has given honor to the dishonorable.

> Nazareth, O Nazareth!
> Tho' name of evil holding,
> There was brought "The Undefiled."
> Like a dove, a serpent folding,
> There grew up "The Holy Child."
> Nazareth! Cross-like we see
> Thy stained name, from all stains free.

These words I have pointed out comprise only a few of the names of our blessed Savior. Meditate on the following names and descriptions:

Second Adam (1 Cor. 15:45–47), Advocate (1 John 2:1), Almighty (Rev. 19:15), Alpha and Omega (Rev. 21:6), Amen (Rev. 3:14), Ancient of Days (Dan. 7:9), Angel of His presence (Is. 63:9), Anointed above His fellows (Ps. 45:7), Anointed of the Lord (Ps. 2:2), Apostle of our profession (Heb. 3:1), Arm of the Lord (Is. 51:9–10), Author and Finisher of our faith (Heb. 12:2),

Babe (Luke 2:16), Beginning and End (Rev. 21:6), Beloved (Eph. 1:6), Beloved of God (Matt. 12:18), Blessed and only Potentate (1 Tim. 6:15), Born of God (1 John 5:18), Branch (Zech. 3:8), Branch of righteousness (Jer. 33:15), Bread of Life (John 6:35), Bridegroom (John 3:29), Captain of Salvation (Heb. 2:10), Carpenter (Mark 6:3), Carpenter's Son (Matt. 13:55), Chief Corner Stone (Ps. 118:22), Chief Shepherd (1 Pet. 5:4), Child (Is. 9:6), Chosen of God (1 Pet. 2:4), Commander (Is. 55:4), Consolation of Israel (Luke 2:25), Counselor (Is. 9:6), Covenant of the people (Is. 42:6), Dayspring (Luke 1:78), Day Star (2 Pet. 1:19), Deliverer (Rom. 11:26), Desire of all nations (Hag. 2:7), Diadem (Is. 28:5), Door (John 10:2), Ensign of the people (Is. 11:10), Eternal Life (1 John 5:20), Everlasting Father (Is. 9:6), Faithful and True (Rev. 19:11), Faithful Witness (Rev. 1:5), Firmly placed Foundation (Is. 28:16), First-begotten (Heb. 1:6), First-born from the dead (Col. 1:18), First Fruits (1 Cor. 15:23), First and Last (Rev. 22:13), Forerunner (Heb. 6:20), Foundation laid in Zion (Is. 28:16), Friend of publicans and sinners (Luke 7:34), God blessed forever (Rom. 9:5), Good Master (Mark 10:17), Great High Priest (Heb. 4:14), Guardian of souls (1 Pet. 2:25), Head of all (Col. 2:10), Head of the body, the church (Col. 1:18), Heir of all things (Heb. 1:2), High Priest (Heb. 4:14), Holy One (1 John 2:20), Holy and Righteous Servant (Acts 3:14), Hope of Glory (Col. 1:27), Horn of Salvation (Luke 1:69), Husband (2 Cor. 11:2), I Am (John 8:58), Image of God (2 Cor. 4:4), Judge of Israel (Mic. 5:1), Just Man (Matt. 27:19), Lamb (Rev. 13:8), Leader (Is. 55:4), Life (John 14:6), Light (John 1:9), Lily of the valleys (Song 2:1), Lion of the tribe of Judah (Rev. 5:5), Man of Peace (Luke 10:6), Man of sorrows (Is. 53:3), Master (Mark 12:14), Mediator (Heb. 12:24), Messenger of the covenant (Mal. 3:1), Mighty God (Is. 9:6), Mighty One of Jacob (Is. 60:16), Minister of the circumcision (Rom. 15:8), Minister of the sanctuary (Heb. 8:1–2), Most Mighty (Ps. 45:3), Only begotten Son (John 1:18), Only wise God (1 Tim. 1:17), Our Passover (1 Cor. 5:7), Our Peace (Eph. 2:14), Physician (Luke 4:23), Power of God (1 Cor. 1:24), Precious Cornerstone (1 Pet. 2:6), Priest (Heb. 5:6), Prince (Acts 5:31), Prophet (Deut. 18:15, 18), Propitiation (Rom. 3:25), Purifer and Refiner (Mal. 3:3), Rabbi (John 6:25), Ransom (1 Tim. 2:6), Redeemer (Is. 59:20), Resurrection and the Life (John 11:25), Righteous Servant (Is. 53:11), Rock (1 Cor. 10:4), Rod of the stem of Jesse (Is. 11:1), Rose of Sharon (Song 2:1), Ruler in Israel (Mic. 5:2), Salvation (Luke 2:30), Scepter out of Israel (Num. 24:17), Second Man (1 Cor. 15:47), Seed of David (John 7:42), Seed of the woman (Gen. 3:15), Shepherd (John 10:11), Shepherd of souls (1 Pet. 2:25), Source of eternal salvation (Heb. 5:9), Sower (Matt. 13:3, 37), Stone rejected (Luke 20:17), Sun of righteousness (Mal. 4:2), Teacher from God (John 3:2), True Vine (John 15:1), Truth (John 14:6), Unspeakable Gift (2 Cor. 9:15), Way (John 14:6), Wonderful (Is. 9:6), Word (John 1:1).

9

The Man of Sorrows

Matthew 23:37-38

I find that one of the conspicuous characteristics of the Bible is its pathos, a feature unmatched in other realms of literature. For power of emotional expression and heart-stirring language, the Scriptures are unsurpassed. Let us compare four striking illustrations from the Old Testament with Jesus' laments over Jerusalem in the New Testament.

There is Jacob's wail of grief: "Me have ye bereaved of my children: Joseph is not, and Simeon is not, and ye will take Benjamin away: all these things are against me" (Gen. 42:36).

Then take the loving entreaty of Ruth: "Intreat me not to leave thee, or to return from following after thee: for whither thou goest, I will go; and whither thou lodgest, I will lodge: thy people shall be my people, and thy God my God: Where thou diest, will I die, and there will I be buried: the LORD do so to me, and more also, if ought but death part thee and me"(Ruth 1:16-17).

Then there is David's heartbroken cry: "O my son Absalom, my son, my son Absalom! would God I had died for thee, O Absalom, my son, my son!" (2 Sam. 18:33). There is also God's yearning pity as expressed by the prophet Hosea: "How shall I give thee up, Ephraim? How shall I deliver thee, Israel?" (Hos. 11:8). Here, in the verses chosen as this chapter's theme, we have Christ's parting wail of rejected love: "O Jerusalem, Jerusalem, thou that killest the prophets, and stonest them which are sent unto thee, how often would I have gathered thy children together, even as a hen gathereth her chickens under her wings, and ye would not! Behold, your house is left unto you desolate" (Matt. 23:37–38). How full of pathos and tragedy is this sob of unwanted love!

The treatment our Lord received during His sojourn here below has been described by John as one of rejection: "He came unto his own, and his own received him not" (John 1:11). Only a small band of followers surrounded Him, and even the best among these did not fully comprehend the truths He taught them.

Here, in Matthew 23:37–38, we confront the rejection of His claims by His own nation. Look at the context. After the lightning flashes of woe, you find the rain of His pity and tears. Three solemn lessons are emphasized in the portion we are considering.

THE STUBBORN SINNER

"O Jerusalem, Jerusalem, thou that killest the prophets, and stonest them which are sent unto thee" (v. 37). The language, as you will notice, is in the present tense— "killest" and "stonest." This tense can include the past, present, and future treatment of both Christ and His own. The past treatment meted out to His representatives is described in the previous verses of this chapter, where our Lord condemns His countrymen for shutting their eyes to the light brought to them by holy messengers.

Then the present treatment He Himself received is pathetically recorded in the words, "often would I . . . ye would not" (v. 37). The words can also apply to the stoning and killing of Stephen, and the martyrdom of almost all the apostles, as well as thousands of the early Christians.

But these words have a practical application to all persons and for all time. They come to us fresh with their pathos and appeal, warning us of the danger of closing heart and life against the Savior. In ignorance and self-will, sinners murder holy thoughts. They slay noble desires and wishes welling up within their hearts. Although some recognize the value and power of Christ's claims, sinners love their sin too much to follow them. And when the sinner closes his eyes to the light, he tramples under his feet the agencies designed for his salvation. Oh, the folly of fighting against godly influences and attempting to banish Christ!

A DISAPPOINTED SAVIOR

Although the Gospels give us several portraits of the Lord Jesus, none is so pathetic and heartbreaking as this. Imagine the sound of these sorrowful words as they left His lips. They contain three glimpses of the love of Him who pleads with men and women to receive Him:

1. He is the Persistent Lover. "*How often* would I have gathered . . ." (v. 37). The intensity of our Savior's feeling can be gathered from the repetition of the name of

the city, "O Jerusalem, Jerusalem" (v. 37). What yearning pity is wrapped up in these words! He looks back
over His own ministry. He thinks of Israel's past history,
when every endeavor was made to make the nation an
example to all the earth. As He gazes at the multiplied
rejections of divine grace and favors, He cries, "How
often would I have gathered thy children." (v. 37). But
such a persistent, heavenly Lover was despised and
rejected.

The tragedy of our day is that careless men and
women are exposed to danger and death and can find it
in their hearts to spurn the Savior's infinite compassion.
Still He strives to gather them under the wings of eternal security.

Are not these words as true of our attitude as that of
the Jews in Christ's own day? Can you hear Him say,
"How often would I have gathered the twentieth-
century secularist under my arms"? Why, He has tried
in a thousand ways to woo and win us from our sin to
Himself—through goodness, sickness, trial, disappointment, death, the ministry of preachers, the influence of
godly friends, the teaching of the Bible, gospel tracts,
and Christ-exalting books. Oh, the persistency of the
Savior, whose love will not let us go! He hopes on to the
very end, with the expectation of seeing us turn to Him.
Therefore, hear it again: If we are finally lost, it will be in
spite of Christ's persistent efforts to save our doomed
souls.

2. He is the Tender Lover. "Even as a hen gathereth
her chickens under her wings" (v. 37). Such a metaphor,
suggesting as it does singular tenderness, proves that
Jesus is compassionate as well as persistent. The nature
of a hen illustrates the great compassion and affection
He had, both for the Jews and for all races. There is no
creature that is moved with so much compassion toward

her young ones as the hen. For example, the hen strives to destroy the forces about to injure her chicks. She will defend them at the utmost hazard to her own life. So Christ endeavors in every possible way to save and defend the sinner against the foes of sin and hell. Yet—and may we take it in!—such loving protection is often despised. The hen, we are told, when the chickens grow up, gives up her care for them. There appears to be a loss of affection. She turns upon them, and they upon her. But Christ never ceases to love, care, and provide for those who receive Him. Although He is treated unkindly, His love is constant and abiding.

When Interpreter of John Bunyan's *Pilgrim's Progress* came into the room where a hen and chickens were, both he and Christiana observed that the hen behaved in a fourfold way toward her chickens. And as Interpreter compared this hen to the King, the chickens to His obedient ones, and the fourfold method of the hen to His dealings towards His people, let us trace the spiritual significance of such a simile.

(1) "She had a Common Call, and that she hath all day long", said Interpreter. So Christ has common call—to everyone—and that all day long. By His common call, said Interpreter, He gives nothing. It is the method whereby He calls attention to Himself. "All day long I have stretched forth my hands unto a disobedient and gainsaying people" (Rom. 10:21).

(2) "She had a Special Call, and that she hath but sometimes." By this call Christ always has something to give. The hen by this special call attracts her chicks for whom she has picked up some dainty morsel. And, Jesus has something specially sweet for you. Yes, and, like the hen, the Savior has also a special call. We hear it when calamities and epidemics are sweeping over the land or when the shadow of death crosses our thresh-

old. My friend, treat such an opportunity as Christ's special call, for He has something to bestow you may never have the chance of receiving again.

(3) "She had a Brooding Note." The hen makes a comforting noise—almost musical—as her young nestle beneath her. It is expressive of her motherly love and desire. Can we not detect something of the passionate yearning of the Savior's heart to gather us under His wings, in that beautiful invitation of His, "Come unto me . . . and I will give you rest" (Matt. 11:28)?

(4) "She had an Outcry." This cry escapes the hen when she sees an enemy approaching. When the hawk or rat is near at hand and her chicks are in danger, the hen quickly warns them. "And," said Interpreter of the King, "He hath an outcry, to give alarm when He seeth the enemy come." Would that I could get multitudes to listen to His outcry, as He desires to shelter them from the hawk of hell, waiting to swoop down on them! "Flee," says the Bible, "from the wrath to come" (Matt. 3:7).

3. He is the Unwanted Lover. "Ye would not" (v. 37). How Jesus lingers wistfully until the bitter end! Why, one can almost catch the sob of His broken heart as these words slowly leave the holy lips of this persistent, tender Lover of souls! "How often would I . . . ye would not" (v. 37). No words more emphatically state the sinner's fatal gift of freedom. You can use your will to frustrate the love, pity, and grace of the Almighty. Or you can yield it up to God until it is sweetly blended with the divine will. The enjoyment of all Christ has depends on the action of your will.

I have been a Christian for over seventy-five years. I have trusted Him. Have you? If I could gather you up in my arms and carry you under His wings, I would willingly do it. But I cannot. If I could give you the grace I have and get more for myself, how eagerly I would help you. Such a bestowal on my part is impossible. You must determine either your salvation or damnation. And because your will is the battleground of decision, may God save you from willingly rejecting Christ as your Savior!

4. He is the Judgmental Lover. "Behold, your house is left unto you desolate" (v. 38). Here our Lord is referring to the nation and the temple within it. As He is about to leave it, He disowns it; it is no longer His. True, the Jews continued to be proud of their house but the Savior had written "Ichabod" (inglorious) over its portals, seeing He had deserted it. And forty years later, both city and temple were abolished. The streets were red with the blood of those very Christ-rejecters.

Surely this teaches us that if we desire security from present evil and future eternal dangers, we must be under Christ's wings. Beware lest your stubborn, willful obstinacy leads Christ to turn from you, as well as you from Him. And if He leaves you to your doom, then death will be a downfall into the unfathomable abyss of unutterable woe. The house of your heart is already desolate if Jesus is not within it. But know that if He is finally excluded from your heart, then eternal desolation will be yours.

The question perplexing many hearts is whether Christ ever takes His final leave of a soul in this world. Somehow I cling to the thought that Jesus pleads and pleads to the end. Yet it may be possible that the utmost punishment for obstinate blindness is the withdrawal of Himself from the sinner's view. "My Spirit shall not always strive with man" (Gen. 6:3) is a Scripture of which to stand in fear.

Do not think you can be saved just when you like, my sinner-friend, for He may leave you alone in darkness.

The saddest punishment of a long-continued rejection of His pleading love is that the soul is unable to respond to the Savior's voice. Who knows? You may be hearing His pleading voice for the last time! You may never hear it again until your godless soul faces Him as the Judge. Hell is full of those who have rejected Him. Beware, then, lest your resistance adds to the number of the desolate! Be persuaded to come under the divine wings for shelter, "Be it known unto you . . . that through this man is preached unto you the forgiveness of sins: And by him all that believe are justified from all things" (Acts 13:38–39).

Consider the words of the poet who compared the setting sun with the Sorrowing Son of Righteousness:

'Tis evening; over Salem's towers a golden lustre gleams,
And lovingly and lingeringly the sun prolongs his beams.
He looks as on some work undone, for which the hour has passed,
So tender is his glance and mild, it seems to be his last.
But a brighter Sun is looking on, more earnest is His eye,
For thunder-clouds must veil Him soon, and darken all the sky:
O'er Zion still He bends, as loath His presence to remove,
And o'er her walls there lingers yet the sunshine of His love.
'Tis Jesus! with an anguished heart, a parting glance He throws,
For mercy's day she has sinned away for a night of dreadful woes:
"Would thou hadst known", He said, while down His face rolled many a tear,
"My words of peace in this thy day—but now thy end is near.
Alas for thee, Jerusalem! How cold thy heart to Me!

How often in these arms of love would I have gathered
thee!
My sheltering wing had been your shield, My love your
happy lot,
I would it had been thus with thee; I would, but ye
would not."
He wept alone, and men passed on—the men whose
woes He bore,
They saw the Man of Sorrows weep, they had seen Him
weep before;
They asked not who those tears were for, they asked not
whence they flowed:
Those tears were for rebellious man, their source the
heart of God.
They fell upon this desert earth like drops from heaven
on high,
Struck from an ocean-tide of love that fill eternity.
With love and tenderness divine those crystal cells
o'erflow:
'Tis God that weeps, through human eyes, for human
guilt and woe!
That hour has fled, those tears are told, the agony is
passed:
The Lord has wept, the Lord has bled, but He has not
loved—His last.
From heaven His eye is downward bent, still ranging to
and fro,
Where'er, in this wild wilderness, there roams a child of
woe;
Nor His alone, the Three in One that looked through
Jesus' eye,
Could still the harps of angel bands to hear the suppliant
sigh;
And when the rebel chooses wrath, God wails his hap-
less lot,
Deep breathing from his heart of love, "I would, but ye
would not."

—John Guthrie

10

The Silent Sufferer

Isaiah 53:7

The fifty-third chapter of Isaiah is the most impressive record of the sufferings of Christ contained in the Bible. Every verse supplies some fresh glimpse of the Crucified; yet the vision was given to the prophet seven hundred years *before* Christ was born. There is nothing more helpful to faith than to go on our knees and read this chapter slowly, praying as we read for the Spirit-inspired Calvary vision. It is only thus that we can enter into the meaning of the death of Him who was smitten of God and afflicted.

Let us look at Isaiah 53:7, which Philip found the eunuch reading (see Acts 8) and from which he preached Christ so effectively as to win the noble African to the Savior. This verse offers two blessed aspects of the vicarious sufferings of Him who was wounded for our transgressions and bruised for our iniquities.

    (1) His Surrender—"He is brought as a lamb to the slaughter."

(2) His Silence—"As a sheep before her shearers is dumb, so he openeth not his mouth."
These two phases of the self-life are hard for most persons to conquer: Self-resistance and self-defense. Reverently, let us examine this verse from the Old Testament prophet of Calvary.

LED AS A LAMB—HIS SURRENDER

The nine words of this phrase are like a string of priceless rubies and offer a rich triad of truth regarding the death of our Lord.
1. His Death Was Voluntary—"He is brought" (or led). Jesus was not forced to His Cross. He was not taken there against His will. He was led! He was oppressed and afflicted! Such language implies His voluntary acceptance of the Cross. He let Himself be afflicted. What amazing grace! He had the power to lay down His life and take it up again, and He did both. O truth sublime! Jesus was not *driven* to Calvary, but *drawn* to it by love to God. His passion was to save a world of sinners lost and ruined by the Fall.
2. His Death Was Vicarious—"As a lamb." Doubtless the prophet had in mind the paschal lamb, offered up instead of the sinful Israelites. Upon the head of the unblemished lamb, a double transfer took place. First the forgiveness of God was assured through the holy lamb, offered and slain. Then the sin of the offerer was removed as he confessed his guilt over the head of the victim.
The knife Abraham believed he should plunge into the heart of Isaac ultimately slew the ram caught in the thicket. The ram died for Isaac; God's Lamb died for me. And is it not strange that this phrase forms the central part of the chapter? Surely it is the central truth of the

gospel! We are redeemed by the precious blood of God's holy Lamb.

3. His Death Was Vicious—"To the slaughter." *Slaughter!* This cruel word suggests the brutality of the death of God's innocent, holy Lamb. Every lamb slain in Isaiah's day died in a humane way, affording the least pain for the innocent animal. But who can measure the shame, indignities, and brutal assaults heaped upon God's Lamb? There was no consideration for His feelings. No wonder nature surrounded the Cross with a robe of darkness, thus covering up the viciousness of human beings as seen in the naked form of the world's Redeemer!

SPEECHLESS AS A SHEEP—HIS SILENCE

This part of the verse describes the greatest heroism ever witnessed by the eyes of men and women. The suffering of innocence is ever nobler than the deserved suffering of guilt. Because of who and what He was, the pang of suffering penetrated the heart of Jesus; yet He held His peace.

Let us glean three further truths regarding His work on behalf of unworthy sinners:

1. His Identification—"As a sheep."

Jesus is often called the Shepherd, but this is the only time He is named a Sheep. And He is both, just as He is Priest and Sacrifice, God and Man. At His baptism, He identified Himself with our fallen race. The climax of this identification was at the Cross, where in some mysterious way He gathered up our sin and made it His own. He was made sin for us! He was numbered with the transgressors! Isaiah tells us that Jesus "made His grave with the wicked, and with the rich in his death" (Is. 53:9). Yes, He died the deaths of all! He tasted death for every person.

2. His Humiliation—"Before her shearers is dumb."
It is an affecting scene to watch a sheep shorn of its
beautiful wool. One always feels a cold shudder of sympathy as one watches a newly-shorn sheep returning to
the field. And as shearers have one aim, namely that of
stripping the sheep of its natural covering, may we not
detect in the figure used by Isaiah a reference to the
deep humiliation of the Savior?

Jesus came before His shearers who stripped Him of
His wool (His clothing), gambling for the possession of
such. "They part my garments among them, and cast
lots upon vesture" (Ps. 22:18). His foes might have had
the decency to leave Him His clothes, but, no, He died
naked, exposed to the cold as well as to shame. Yes, and
His nakedness was a type of the sinner's wretchedness,
who naked, comes to Him for dress. Sheep give their
wool that others might be covered. The wool suits and
dresses we sometimes wear represent the surrender of a
multitude of sheep. And so the humiliation, shame, and
stripping of the Savior provide the warm, eternal robe of
righteousness and salvation for all mankind.

3. His Self-abnegation—"He openeth not his mouth."
This brings us to the glorious victory of Christ over His
anguish and shame. If you watch a sheep being shorn—
or even slain—you will find that it submits most silently.
Three times over Isaiah tells us in this verse that Jesus
was silent. Twice we read, "he opened [openeth] not his
mouth"; once, that He was "dumb." And such fits in
with the three occasions the Savior was silent when
facing His enemies: (1) before the Jewish rulers, Jesus
held His peace (see John 18:1–27); (2) facing Pilate, He
answered almost nothing (see John 18:33–19:11); and (3)
before Herod, He made no reply (see Luke 23:7–9).

He could have loudly protested His innocence. One
breath from Him would have slain all those who clam-
ored for His blood, even as they had been stricken to the

ground at the sight of Him in Gethsemane. But by His attitude, our blessed Lord not only manifested the surrender of self, in that He allowed cruel men to lead Him out to His death; He demonstrated also the silence of self, in that He never uttered one word in His defense, although He knew that He was hated without a cause. The reason He suffered in silence was that He knew that Calvary was the will of God the Father for Him. Although His death was not deserved, it was decreed. It pleased the Lord to bruise Him! The psalmist answers this mystery in the words, "I was dumb, I opened not my mouth; because thou didst it" (Ps. 39:9). He endured the Cross, despising the shame, and is now seated at the right hand of God the Father.

What death to self-defense! What an example to us! Here, then, are two avenues of victory if we care to follow our smitten, silent Lord. Are we willing to be led as lambs and be silent as sheep?

LED AS LAMBS

A lamb is a young sheep. Because Jesus died at the early age of thirty-three, He claims all the powers of youth. A lamb is the emblem of innocency, activity, and freshness. May God give us grace to lead our lambs to the altar, even as Abraham led Isaac!

There is another application, however, of this phrase. Often we render a good deal of forced work in our service for the Lord and act under compulsion. Our Christian life and work is a treadmill existence. We lack the lamblike character of submission and willing surrender. We shrink from the slaughter! We save ourselves! We are not willing to be "accounted as sheep for the slaughter" (Rom. 8:36), as Paul puts it. O for grace to die to our own will and way and to be led as lambs!

SILENT AS SHEEP

Peter tells us that in Jesus' silence, He left us an example to follow. Although "he was reviled, reviled not again; when He suffered, he threatened not." (1 Pet. 2:23). But do we follow His steps in such silent submission? How do we act when we come before our shearers? Are we silent or assertive, dumb or defensive? When we are shorn of our reputation, position, place, or office, how do we act? Do we raise our voice in defense and stoutly contend for our rights, giving our shearers a piece of our mind?

The Calvary way is silence! We moan, "But, O Lord, it is a hard and difficult road for our feet to travel!" We like to protest our innocence. And the only answer to our cry is, that He was innocent. His death was the greatest blunder ever made; yet He allowed it, enduring the cruel, unjust judgment and bitterness of the cross— silent! We love to fight, argue, claim our rights, and show people that we are not to be sat on. Jesus held His peace!

Yes, and when it comes to the slaughter of our ambitions and to the shearing of many dear things in life, it may be hard to accept such as part of God's will. Yet as we walk the blood-red way, it is wonderful to see Him justifying our surrender and silence.

How many there are who are dumb, opening not their mouths amid the mysterious dealings of God! I honor these silent sufferers! Have you not met many of them on life's journey? Mothers, heavily laden with the care of the home, yet never murmuring. Pain-stricken, diseased, lonely souls who never complain or rebel. Noble hearts, who although misjudged and treated adversely, suffer in silence, drinking deeply of the spirit of the silent Sufferer of Calvary. I hope that you and I will be found in such august company!

11

The Open Door of an Empty Grave

Christians don't shun Calvary; they make the place their home of comfort on this earth. The house of consolation is built with the wood of the cross of Jesus. The temple of heavenly blessing is founded upon a riven Rock—riven by the spear of the soldier that pierced the heart of our Redeemer. Truly there is no scene in sacred history that has the power to gladden the soul like Calvary's dark tragedy, when viewed through the open door of an empty tomb. "Come, see the place where the Lord lay" (Matt. 28:6).

In life's sorrowful hours, thoughts of Gethsemane and Calvary alleviate our sufferings and woes. As one of our spiritual poets has expressed it:

> Is it not strange, the darkest hour
>   That ever dawned on sinful earth,
> Should touch the heart with softer power
>   For comfort, than an angel's mirth?
> That to the Cross the mourner's eye upward turns,
> Sooner than where the star of Bethlehem burns?

Let us turn anew to that sweet resting place of His, once the agonies of the bitter cross are over. Processions to newly dug graves are solemn and sacred occasions. As we stand there, remembering our precious dead, we have heavenly and holy thoughts. After death, visits are frequent to God's green acre where the bodies of our loved ones sleep. Yes, *sleep,* and this is why we have the name *cemetery,* meaning a sleeping place. And such it is, seeing that the precious dust of the dead must sleep therein until the resurrection morn.

But we cannot visit too frequently the grave where the body of Jesus has lain. May heaven forbid that our journeys should become less or that we should ungratefully forget His death! Let us keep the fact of this grave ever fresh in our memories, allowing it to intensify our love for Him who robbed death of its prey. This is why the Master instituted the memorial feast bearing His name. What would we think of a bereaved wife who never went to her husband's grave, there to silently remember him as her lover and friend? Why, we would call her a callous creature; a heartless, ungrateful widow! By her attitude, she would suggest that the attachment was not very deep and real.

Yet there are those who never remember the death of their Lord in His appointed, yea, commanded, way. Such neglect must grieve His heart. And further, no matter how we may theologically wiggle out of the observance of the Lord's Supper, the fact remains that every Christian who fails to participate in it is guilty of the sin of direct disobedience. Such nonobservance is as heartless as the widow's neglecting her loved one's grave.

Several truths come to our remembrance when we think of the sacred sepulcher wherein our Master was buried:

1. It was a *grave.* Such a common end tells us that

Jesus came and lived a human life, passed through human experiences, and apparently had the usual end. "Low in a grave He lay—Jesus, my Savior!"

Both the music of a baby's cry and the moans of a dying man came from His lips. He had a death as well as a birth; a grave as well as a cradle; a shroud as well as the swaddling clothes. But His was not a grave on some lonely windswept moor, as many a desert traveler and covenanter has found. It was in a garden, bright with the flowers of spring and decked with the beauties of nature. Here, then, is the origin of the symbolic custom of carrying flowers to the grave.

Christ's grave in a garden was a type or parable of grace. It tells me that if I will but accept Him as my Savior and love Him as my Lord, then my grave of sin and despair will become a garden of lovely flowers. If I come to His grave, burying therein my sin and self-will, if I drop like a corn of wheat into His sepulcher and die, then I have the promise that my life will bring forth flowers and fruit, both beautiful and bounteous. The grave speaks of death; the garden, of resurrection. Ere long our graves will become gardens when the dead in Christ shall be raised and the living shall be changed.

2. It was a *new* grave. Joseph's "own new tomb" (Matt. 27:60), one "wherein never man before was laid" (Luke 23:53) are the descriptions given of Christ's resting place for three days. Thus He who was borne within the virgin womb of Mary, was at last buried within the virgin tomb of Joseph—a fitting grave, was it not, for Him who had lived a virgin life? But such a coincidence proclaims the fact that Jesus must be first, or as Paul expresses it, have the place of preeminence in all things. He must have the best, unstained and untouched by sin. This same principle is seen in His use of the colt "whereon yet never man sat" (Luke 19:30).

Furthermore, Joseph's new grave was befitting for

the Lord who was about to do a new thing in the world's history, namely, conquer the Devil who had and still has mystifying power. By His death and resurrection, He made an end of sin and prepared for us an everlasting righteousness. This is the message of His new and empty grave: "Behold, I make all things new" (Rev. 21:5). True, there have been millions of graves both before and since His new tomb, but Christ's grave was unique in that it contained the crucified body of the God-man. Although without sin, He was made sin for us upon Calvary's cross. Having finished the work which the Father gave Him to do, His body was buried in a new tomb.

3. It was a *borrowed* grave. The prophet Isaiah tells us that Jesus "made his grave with the wicked, and with the rich in his death." (Is. 53:9) His rich grave, however, was a borrowed one. Most people, unless they are paupers, have graves of their own in which to be buried. Christ's is a stranger's grave—a fitting conclusion to His life of humiliation. The wonder of His condescension is that although a Creator, He became utterly dependent upon His creatures. For example: He was born in a stable not His own, dined at another man's table, slept in another man's boat—He had no place of His own in which to rest His weary head. Now for three days He lies buried in another man's grave.

Such facts proclaim the depths of Christ's humiliation for us. He had nothing of His own. Where can we find another so fully dependent both upon man, as well as the Father, as He?

Let it not be forgotten that although Joseph gave Christ his own new tomb, he really gave Him that which was His own. Our possessions are not ours but His. By his gracious act, Joseph was saying: "Lord, my tomb is Thine; the rock forming it was fashioned by Thee; the garden in which it was placed was kissed into beauty by Thy power. Take it! The cost of preparing it is nothing in comparison with the depth of Thy sacrifice for me." Joseph realized, even as we should, that all he possessed was like his new tomb—borrowed. So when we minister to Him of ourselves and our substance, we but give Him of His own.

4. It was a *disciple's* grave. Someone would have to bury the sacred body of Jesus. If not, the birds of the air would devour His flesh. His bones would bleach and rot. So it came to pass that the honor of housing Christ's dead body fell to Joseph, the rich man of Arimathaea and a secret disciple of Jesus. And by his gracious act, he lurked no longer in secrecy but declared to all that he loved the One buried in his tomb. Yes, and having given nobly and unselfishly his own well-prepared grave to his Master, he would revere Him forever after.

It is somewhat strange that Jesus was associated with two Josephs—one at either end of His short yet active course. At the beginning there was Joseph the carpenter, a poor laboring man who gave Jesus a loving but humble home as He entered the world. And then at the end, there was Joseph of Arimathaea, a rich man who surrendered His beautiful grave for Jesus to rest in as He left the world. Thus Jesus received homage from the poor and rich. Although born in a stable, He was buried in a costly grave. Both of these men lodged the Savior and befriended Him, when He was despised and rejected by others. The Babe found no room in the inn, and His life was threatened by Herod the King; but Joseph heard the call of God, "Arise, and take the young child" (Matt. 2:13), and he lovingly cared for Him. Then at the end of Christ' life, when cruelly martyred as the unwanted King and sent out of the world as a felon, another Joseph was ready to care for His remains.

He is still the unwanted One, and He yearns for more Josephs to give Him a resting place. Will your heart be His home, your money His possession? True, He no longer requires a manger or a tomb, for all such necessities are past for Him. But He does desire you to shield Him in your heart from the scorn of a bitter world and to trust all you own to His use. If others have no place for Him, then you must endeavor to hide Him, even as one Joseph did in his home and the other Joseph in his tomb.

5. It was an *empty* grave. It is a glorious fact that the women found the grave of Christ empty. "Come, see the place where the Lord lay" (Matt. 28:6). Yes, although my Lord was once entombed, He broke the shackles and forsook that prison house of death. Listen to Peter's victorious word: "Whom God hath raised up, having loosed the pains of death" (Acts 2:24). Some there are who chant the mournful creed:

> Now He is dead! For here He lies,
> In a lone Syrian town;
> And on His grave, with shining eyes,
> The Syrian stars look down.

But our faith is expressed otherwise and triumphantly sings:

> Up from the grave He arose,
> With a mighty triumph o'er his foes.

His empty grave preaches three sublime truths to the believer: First, the Father was well pleased with His Son's obedience and with His sacrifice. Now, because of His Son's death, God makes the believer welcome to His heart and home. Second, Christ's resurrection is the pledge to the believer's soul that the risen Master can bestow a life of holiness by the power of the life-giving

Spirit. In the third place, the empty grave is a prophecy of that day when all who sleep in Jesus will follow Him out of their graves into joy unspeakable.

No wonder Bunyan shouted as he viewed the empty tomb, "Blessed sepulcher!" It is indeed a significant, blessed grave. We cannot resort to it too often, delight in it too ardently, revere it too solemnly, declare it too loyally. It is empty!

How fervently the apostle Paul declares: "But now is Christ risen from the dead, and become the first fruits of them that slept. For since by man came death, by man came also the resurrection of the dead" (1 Cor. 15:20–21).

To the apostle John on the isle of Patmos, the Lord of glory said: "Fear not, I am the first and the last, and the living one; I died, and behold I am alive for evermore, and I have the keys of Death and Hades" (Rev. 1:17–18, RSV).

12

The Savior of Souls

Haven't these previous chapters said *everything* that needs to be said about the Nazarene? Haven't we traveled in this study *all the way* from His divinely foretold birth to His empty, victorious tomb?

Dear friend, there is more. I want to take you, finally, to the neglected truth of the Second Coming. But before we reach that stopping place, I need to put before you the claims of the Savior. It is my purpose to remind you of the preeminence of the Lord Jesus as the Savior of souls. Remember Hebrews 7:25: "He is able also to save them to the uttermost that come unto God by him, seeing he ever liveth to make intercession for them."

You and I have the obligation, as well as the great joy, of pressing the claims of the Savior upon all unbelievers. We have learned what He can mean to our lives because of who He is.

Truly He is unique and superb, mighty and majestic. There has never been His like, for the Lord Jesus Christ revealed Himself not only as the man Jesus but as very God of very God. He stands in a category all His own; solitary yet sublime.

Because we have experienced His saving grace, we love to declare His greatness. As you know, He is the Lord God Almighty. His greatness is the dominant fact of Holy Writ. The truth of His exalted position runs like a golden thread through the Word of God. You can never lose sight of His greatness and charm as you study the blessed Book. Even in its final pages, in the Book of the Revelation, He is displayed as the First and the Last, and all in between.

Another incentive, I think, urging us to proclaim the pre-eminence of the Lord is the apostasy surrounding us in these modern days. The secularist denies the uniqueness and supernaturalness of His person, tries to cripple His omnipotence, and seeks to reduce Him to the level of ordinary humanity. What blatant impudence to declare that Jesus Christ is a man—a good man, maybe, but only a man! True, He became the Son of Man, but He was never the son of *a* man.

Your conception of His magnificence and greatness determines the quality of your life. Low views of His worth lead to low living. Faith in Him as the pre-eminent Lord must lead to a pre-eminent life—one with priorities. The conception of the Lordship of the Redeemer delivers you from anxiety. If you are tempted to worry about needs, whether they be spiritual or material, the thought of the Savior as the marvelous One slays all doubt. There is nothing that can kill doubt in the life of a saint like the understanding of the truth that Job proclaimed—"I know that thou canst do every thing" (Job 42:2).

Again, realization of the Lordship of the Redeemer destroys the fear of persons and things. When we believe that He is greater than all—He is the Lord God Omnipotent—then we learn how to look away even from our outward circumstances. We do not fear sin or

Satan or the powers of darkness or mere, weak, puny human beings. We realize that we have a mighty Savior. And this is why Peter tells us to cast all our cares upon Him, for angels and authorities and powers are subject unto Him (see 1 Pet. 5:7).

What else can we do but declare His saving grace when we know that He is supreme within the realm of salvation? "Beside me there is no savior" (Is. 43:11). And He has amply justified that claim, as the experience of a vast multitude of redeemed souls can testify. Consider the question, "Who is a God like unto thee, that pardoneth iniquity?" (Mic. 7:18).

Jesus Christ is incomparable as the Savior of souls. He is matchless in extricating sin-cursed lives out of the clutches of the monarch of hell.

1. HE CAN SAVE ANY NUMBER

As we study the infallible Word of God, it is with joy that we trace the power of the Lord Jesus in the realm of salvation. First of all, Jesus Christ is able to save any number. Jonathan's confident word is true of the Savior in a very deep sense: "There is no restraint to the LORD to save by many or by few" (1 Sam. 14:6). Omnipotence never stops at numbers.

The system of heaven's arithmetic is totally different from ours. Thus, as the greater includes the lesser, Jesus Christ is able to save any quantity, as the Bible proves. For example, He can save persons one by one. Our Lord believed in personal evangelism; thus Andrew and Peter and others were brought to Him in that way. Some of the most remarkable utterances falling from the lips of the Lord Jesus are found in those brief, private conversations of His.

Some of the greatest workers in the vineyard of the

Lord today were won individually—a saved soul spoke to another about the things that matter most. And the Lord has a way of dealing with persons separately. He lays hold of a person and deals with that *one* as if there were no other.

He has power to save many at the same time, for we read that many of the Samaritans believed. We are not told how many there were in that company. But all of them responded spontaneously to the appeal of the changed woman as she found her way back from the well (see John 4:28–29). And so by His Spirit the Lord can breathe on any given assembly, making all within the gathering receptive to His power.

He has power to save a multitude with the same ease that He can deliver the individual. We read that, on the day of Pentecost, three thousand were brought under the sway of the Spirit. What a marvelous display of His power that was! We have had similar manifestations of His power in the history of the church. Think of that African Pentecost, when, through the ministry of Dr. Charles Inwood, 2,500 souls were bowed under the power of the Spirit of God at one time.

With equal power, Christ can save a nation, for we read that a nation is to be born again in a day (see Is. 66:8). The time is coming when He will move upon His scattered people and regather them, and as a nation refashion them in a moment of time.

Let me summarize: He can save individuals; He can save many at one time; He can save a multitude with the same ease; He can save a nation just as simply.

2. HE CAN SAVE ANYWHERE

I discover from my study of the Word of God that Jesus Christ can save anywhere. He is not only omnipotent, but He is also omnipresent. He is no respecter of places. His eyes run to and fro throughout the whole earth. He is the center and circumference of all things. Location is unlimited for Him. He fills all space; so, wherever Christ is, there is salvation. Said He to Zacchaeus, "This day is salvation come to this house" (Luke 19:9), and salvation entered the home of Zacchaeus on two feet. Salvation is not an object, a mere possession—it is a Person. "He only is . . . my salvation" (Ps. 62:2).

Let us discover how Jesus Christ is able to save anywhere. He saved one man in a custom house—for that was where He found Levi the tax-gatherer. And Levi is not the only man whom Jesus has met and saved at a desk.

He can save by the seaside. That is where He found Peter and the other hard-working fishermen who responded to His call. Others go to the beach not to work but to relax. Many there are who have found Jesus while on vacation. On the sands at Brighton, Hudson Taylor met God face to face. That crisis in his spiritual history resulted in the birth of the China Inland Mission.

Jesus can save in a house. That is where the paralytic man was healed and forgiven. And how many have found the Lord Jesus by their own fireside? Years ago in Glasgow, while having some special meetings in Bethany Hall, the "sister" hall of Tent Hall, I heard a man in a testimony meeting say that he had been born twice in the same bed. That mystified me until he explained. In the very same bed where he had first seen the light of day, many years later, during a time of sickness, he saw the light of eternity in Christ.

Jesus Christ can save souls at the foot of a tree, for that is where Zacchaeus saw Jesus. A friend in Scotland found Christ beneath a wonderful tree on the roadside.

He never journeys that way without stopping and bending his knees at the foot of that tree to thank God for the day when he found Jesus. Really, all sinners who would be saved must journey to a tree—even the cross upon which the Master died.

Jesus is able to save in the middle of the road, for that is where Saul of Tarsus was found of Him. The Samaritan woman is another open-air convert. We thank God for those saved by grace through the influence of open-air meetings. He can save in a pool, for that is where the man of Bethesda found the healing mercy of the Redeemer. Martin Luther, climbing the steps of a sanctuary, learned the blessed truth concerning justification by faith. With equal power He is able to save in the heart of a desert, for that is where, through Philip, He found the Ethiopian eunuch. He can save in a prison, for that is where, through Paul, He found the jailer. Many there are who, while behind bars, have come to know the grace of God.

While a student in the Bible Training Institute of Glasgow, it was my privilege to have a class in Barlinnie Prison. There I had the joy of seeing what God was able to do among criminals. A young man found Jesus there in the prison cell. After being released, he secured a situation in a Glasgow institution I know very well. One day, he died very suddenly.

At his grave, five ex-convicts, all men who had found Christ in prison, lowered the remains of that young man into his resting place.

When the funeral was over, a friend secured the Testament that had belonged to this young man. In it were found written the words that formed his testimony: "O Nazarene, Thou hast conquered by an infinitude of love, and if out of the wreckage of my life Thou canst make character that will abide, I choose to follow Thee." Yes, Jesus Christ can save in a prison.

He can save on a cross, for that is where the malefactor came to know the Lord's forgiveness. And I suppose if our spiritual experiences could be written, it would be found that we met Christ in all kinds of places. So He is able to save anywhere, in a ghetto or a condo, on the street or in the sanctuary, on land or sea or in the air—it makes no difference to Him. "Whither shall I flee from thy presence?" (Ps. 139:7).

3. HE CAN SAVE AT ANY TIME

Jesus Christ can save at any time. We are told that He never slumbers nor sleeps, that He is ever on the alert to save the lost. His eyes are ever open, beholding the need of the Christless, and His hands are ever ready to deliver.

I discovered while meditating on this theme, that the three thousand were converted at the third hour of the day, which is nine o'clock in the morning. Revival is not bound by time. Saul was converted at midday, the noon hour. The thief was saved between the sixth and the ninth hour (twelve o'clock to three o'clock in the afternoon). John met Christ at the tenth hour, which is four o'clock in the afternoon. Nicodemus found Jesus at night. I, myself, found Him at 9:15 one evening. The jailer found Christ at the midnight hour. So, from midday to midnight, Jesus never wearies seeking out the lost. He is not restrained by time. He does not judge His movements by the hands of the clock, as we usually do. As we face men and women let us tell them that they cannot be saved in their own time and whenever they like, but only in God's time. And God's time is now. "Now is the accepted time; behold, now is the day of salvation" (2 Cor. 6:2).

4. HE CAN SAVE AT ANY AGE

My Bible teaches me that Jesus Christ is able to save at any age. From the first dawn of accountable action until life's closing period, He is able to deliver. Such is His grace that He can adapt Himself to the needs of every season of life.

He can save children. Thus it was that little Samuel came to know the Lord. Jesus Himself said: "Suffer the little children to come unto me, and forbid them not: for of such is the kingdom of God" (Mark 10:14). And we should labor to bring these dear children in life's fair morning to Christ, for then the Lord bestows upon them a double salvation—a soul is saved and a life secured for the One who is pre-eminent as the Savior.

Jesus Christ is able to save youth. A rich young ruler came to Jesus concerned about moral ideas, but, like a good many of today's young men and women, he was not prepared to pay the price of a full and unreserved surrender to the claims of Jesus Christ. Now, if it be true that youth is life's most beautiful moment, we must urge young men and women to receive the Savior and indicate that He has a divine claim upon their lives.

He can save the old. Nicodemus, as an aged man, learned that truth, for said he to Jesus, "How can a man be born when he is old?" (John 3:4). No wonder he asked that question, for it does seem difficult for old people to respond to the appeal of the Savior. The neglect of years settles down upon them, and the hinges of the heart are rusted with unbelief. One of the tragedies of the Gospel is this fact: Few old people are found wending their way to the feet of the Crucified. And yet, by His power, these men and women can be born again no matter their age. "Him that cometh to me I will in no wise cast out" (John 6:37).

Then, He can save at the end of life, for that is when the dying thief came to know the Savior's power. At the eleventh hour, nay, on the stroke of twelve, He is able to save!

5. HE CAN SAVE ANY CHARACTER

Jesus Christ is able to save any character. We are reminded here of the question of the disciples, "Who then can be saved?" (Matt. 19:25). Bless His name, He is no respecter of persons. He can save to the utmost. Our Lord pays no attention to the superficial divisions of society. He knows only one class, and everyone is in it: "All have sinned, and come short of the glory of God" (Rom. 3:23). "And I, if I be lifted up from the earth, will draw all men unto me" (John 12:32).

Let us see how this can be true. Can He save any character? Yes, He can save a harlot like Rahab and the sin-stained woman of Samaria. Jesus Christ stands out as the emancipator of debauched womanhood and manhood as well. He can take men and women from the gutter, as He did Billy Sunday and Mel Trotter, and place them among the princes and princesses of God. He can save demon-possessed women like Mary Magdalene and the young girl possessed with a spirit of divination. He can save a moral man like Nathanael. He can save a religious man like Nicodemus. He can save a rich man like Zacchaeus. True, "not many wise men after the flesh . . . not many noble, are called" (1 Cor. 1:26), but thank God, some are called and come to know what it is to fling their possessions and their wealth at His feet.

He can save a poor man like Lazarus the beggar. Poverty and riches form no criteria, for we are not saved because of what we may have but because of what we are. And this is where I part company with any movement that has a gospel primarily for rich and prominent people. Jesus Christ pays no attention to divisions of society. He, of course, went to the poor.

With equal power He can save fishermen; so you find Peter and others responding to His appeal. How we thank God for Jock Troup, a one-time fisherman brought under the power of the gospel and used of God in a remarkable way as His weapon of war and battle-ax.

He can save a doctor. We read of Luke the physician, and we bless Him for those who in this sacred vocation of life have had thrilling experiences of His deliverance. We think of Sir James Simpson, the discoverer of chloroform, who declared that his greatest discovery of life was the fact that he was a sinner and Jesus Christ was able to save. We think of a convert of D. L. Moody's, Sir Wilfred Grenfell, who as a physician accomplished mighty things for God along the coasts of Labrador.

He is able to save a high government official; so you find the eunuch in the desert seeking the Savior. By the way, that episode in the desert declared that Jesus Christ pays no attention to color, for Philip was a white man, and the eunuch was probably a black man. But they traveled together, musing upon the Savior's marvelous power.

He can save a tent-maker; so we read of Priscilla and Aquila and Saul of Tarsus. He can save a tax-gatherer; so we have the conversion of Levi. He can save even a lawyer; so we read of Zenas. He can save a working woman; so we learn of Lydia, who was a seller of purple. He can save a jailer; so we have the story of grace in that Philippian prison. He can save a thief; so we have the record of the malefactor who believed in Jesus in his dying moment.

Thus He is able to save all kinds of sinners; therefore, why should you or your friends despair? Whether they be vicious or virtuous, whether they be princes or paupers, all kinds of persons can come to the Savior.

> While grace is offered to the prince,
>   The poor may take their share;
> No mortal has a just pretense
>   to perish in despair.
> None are excluded hence, but those
>   Who do themselves exclude;
> Welcome the learned and polite,
>   The ignorant and rude.

And so, as the result of this study on Christ's ability to save, let us press the trumpet of salvation to our lips and herald this faithful saying, worthy of all acceptation: That Jesus Christ is able to save anywhere, at any age, and under all circumstances. God the Father loves souls. Jesus Christ died for souls. And the Spirit pleads for souls. The Word of God invites souls. Angels wait to rejoice over souls. Therefore, may it be our passion to win souls. By all means may we save some!

13

The One Who Promised to Return

Do you thrill to hear a soloist sing "The King Is Coming"? Study God's Word, and I think you will decide that marvelous event will happen soon.

The glorious hope of every Christian is the bodily return of our Lord. All of history will find its culmination in the events that quickly follow the Second Coming. For everyone, saint and sinner alike, all the loose ends will be tied up. The Christian will be rewarded; the sinner will be punished. All of these matters will begin with the event that could occur with the next tick of the clock.

The doctrine should not seem strange. It is natural. It should not be separated from the rest of Jesus' teachings.

Closely allied to the theme of the kingdom is what the Master taught regarding His Second Coming. When, according to His promise, He returns to translate His church to glory, events will accelerate until they culminate in the Millennium. Then He will personally reign "where'er the sun doth his successive journeys run."

Then "every creature will rise and bring, peculiar honors to our king."

The future, both near and far off, loomed large in the teaching of Jesus. His eyes ever beheld the land of far distances. Priority, however, is given to what Jesus accomplished during his first coming since that forms the basis of all He will make us the recipients of at His Second Coming. "*First of all* . . . Christ died for our sins according to the scriptures" (1 Cor. 15:3, italics added). Jesus Himself declared that He came among sinners to give His life as a ransom for their sin.

Nothing that has happened in the long history of the world can compare to all that was involved in the Incarnation, the great historic fact upon which our Christian faith and hope rest. Next in importance is the teaching of Jesus in His predicted and promised return for His redeemed church and for His universal reign on earth as the King of nations. This is why His appearing is referred to as the *Second Coming,* the word *second* being used to differentiate between His coming in humility and His return in glory as the King of Kings.

There are those, however, who quibble about the phrase, affirming that the Bible nowhere speaks of a *Second* Coming, but only of *the* coming or appearing. But this contention is entirely wrong, for the Bible *does* use the word *second* in connection with Christ's return. "Christ was *once* offered to bear the sins of many; and unto them that look for him shall he appear the *second* time without sin unto salvation" (Heb. 9:28, italics added). His words, "come again," (John 14:3) surely mean a second time!

Whenever Jesus dealt with the topic of eschatology (last things), He knew what He was talking about and made the truth clear and plain, which is more than some theologians are able to do when they seek to expound what He taught. The hymn rebukes us by saying that "if our love were but more simple, we would take him at his word."

In the four Gospels, Jesus mentions His return almost twenty times. The earliest reference was when He sent out the twelve to preach the gospel, saying, "Ye shall not have gone over the cities of Israel, till the Son of man be come" (Matt. 10:23). From then on, He gave promises concerning His return and made frequent predictions of events leading up to and associated with such an event. In His last reference, before He died, to His Second Coming, He gave His own the warning: "Watch therefore, for ye know neither the day nor the hour wherein the Son of man cometh" (Matt. 25:13). Jesus laid great stress upon the duty of watchfulness in view of His promised coming.

The Greek word for *coming* is *parousia* and usually implies "arrival and presence." Some verses give prominence to the period of time concept, and others, to the arrival aspect. This term *parousia* is also used to denote the coming or appearance of the Antichrist (see 2 Thess. 2:9). (Another expression Paul uses is *apokálupsis*, which depicts Christ's appearance in majesty and glory, His "uncovering of glory.") *Parousia*, implying "presence" as opposed to "absence," not only denotes the return of Jesus at the end of the gentile age, but also His promised return to take His own to be with Him where He presently is (see John 14:1-4). And this brings us to a consideration of what is actually meant by the phrase *Second Coming*.

Within the general term *Second Coming* are many events which must be distinguished. Otherwise confusion will reign, as, alas! it does in the minds of many who fail to separate aspects that differ. It is, of course, best not to cloud the hope of His coming with too detailed a theory as to what will transpire when He returns. Probably there will be those dear hearts who will be disappointed if Jesus does not follow the schedule they have clearly mapped out for Him.

On the other hand, it is just as unwise not to study the various events and say, "Well, He's coming again, and that's enough for me." We are urged, are we not, to be diligent, "rightly dividing the word of truth" (2 Tim. 2:15)? Unprofitable speculation we shun, but a sane interpretation we welcome.

The reader will understand that for a complete exposition of *all* that is implied in the appearance of Jesus the second time, it is necessary to trace such a glorious theme as a whole through the entire New Testament. But we are confining ourselves in this final chapter to what the Master taught. After all, He is the one who is coming, and His teaching on the subject is therefore supreme and authoritative.

That the world owes much to the latest utterances of its eminent saints can be gathered from my work on *Last Words of Saints and Sinners*. While *all* the sayings of Jesus are of deep importance and gather and grow in intensity as He nears His end, His later promises and predictions are most precious and of deepest importance. He Himself came into the foreground; He became the great theme of His farewell sayings. Somehow His insights grew more exalted as His way grew more troubled. The shadow that fell upon His spirit was marked by a correspondent change in His teaching. He became sadder in speech as in soul—the Man of Sorrows, despised and rejected of men. The gathering clouds, however, left His outlook clear. The larger part of His great discourse of future events in connection with His coming again was given within a few days of His death (see Matt. 24:1–26:2).

In John's Gospel, the public ministry of Jesus seems to end with the twelfth chapter. Thereafter, His last words were to His own (see John 13:1). Knowing that His trial and crucifixion would stun His disciples almost out of their faith, He purposely dwelt on those truths that would solidify their hopes of Him in a far grander way than they had ever yet dreamed.

In a chapter, "The Later Teaching," Fairbairn gives us a most heart-moving description of the peculiarities that distinguish the latter teaching of Jesus. In fact, these paragraphs are without parallel in spiritual literature.

> We can hardly approach the final words of Christ without reverence. As we study them we almost feel as if we were overhearing His speech, or looking into His spirit, or watching the ebb and flow of emotion on His wondrous face. . . . His words have been a source of infinite wonder to the world, a kind of divine heart and conscience in it. They are but few; we can read in an hour all of His thought that survives, which the forms of human art have created to clothe and immortalize the human spirit.
>
> Nor was He careful to preserve them, wrote no word, commanded no word to be written; spoke, as it were, into the listening air the words it was to hear and preserve for all time. And speech thus spoken into the air has been like a sweet and subtle divine essence in the heart of humanity . . . . Had the words of Christ vanished into silence, passed into the great halls of oblivion, or had they never been spoken, our world had been quite other than it is, and been far from as wise and good as it is now. So great and infinite in value have been those teachings, in quantity smallest of fragments, in quality greatest and most priceless of the treasures that have enriched the World.

By cataloging a few of these final Advent utterances, we can discover the related events.

"If I go and prepare a place for you, I will come again, and receive you unto myself" (John 14:3).

"I will not leave you comfortless: I will come to you" (John 14:18).

"He cometh in the glory of his Father with the holy angels" (Mark 8:38).

"They shall see the Son of man coming in a cloud with power and great glory" (Luke 21:27).

"As it was in the days of Lot . . . . even thus shall it be in the day when the Son of man is revealed" (Luke 17:28,30).

"The Son of man shall come in the glory of his Father with his angels" (Matt. 16:27).

"When the Son of man shall come in his glory, and all the holy angels with him" (Matt. 25:31).

When the hour dawns for Jesus to leave the Father's home on His triumphant journey back to earth, He will not descend all the way without a break. Two features or events are related to His coming, namely, the *reception of the church* and the *reign of Christ*, with several events leading up to the latter.

We are cognizant of the fact that prophecy suffers many wounds in the house of its friends. Conflicting interpretations cause many to leave such an entrancing theme alone. Some there are who clump all events together, making no distinction as to their nature or time. All recorded promises concerning the Second Coming will be fulfilled when Jesus appears as the august Judge at the Last Judgment.

What Jesus promised His disciples about returning for and receiving them, however, is in a category of its own. The phrase, "I will come again, and receive you unto myself" (John 14:3), must imply a *personal* return for not only the disciples who listened to the tender words of Jesus, but for all believers. Those original believers formed the church in representation. There is to be an entrance for His church which He said He would build into an eternal communion with Himself. There are those who make the promise of Jesus to mean either His coming in judgment upon Jerusalem in A.D

70, or the coming of the Holy Spirit on the Day of Pentecost, or His coming at death to take the believer to be with himself. But I am simple enough to believe that when he said "I will come again," He meant He, Himself—not the Spirit—would come in final glory.

RECEPTION OF THE CHURCH

To all who have received Him as a personal Savior (see John 1:12), He will receive them unto Himself when He appears the second time. This royal reception will take place on His way to take His power and reign. The testimony of the two heavenly visitants was that "This same Jesus, which is taken up from *you* into heaven, shall so come *in like manner* as *ye* have seen him go into heaven" (Acts 1:11, italics added). How did He go? In the presence of His own (see Acts 1:9–10). How will He return? In the same manner, in the presence of His own. We differentiate between His coming *for* His church and His coming *with* her.

Presently, we have the church triumphant in heaven and the church militant on earth. The former Jesus will bring *with* Him, while the latter—"we which are alive and remain" (1 Thess. 4:15)—will be immediately transformed and translated to meet the Lord with the glorified host in the air, to which Paul says we are to be "caught up" (1 Thess. 4:17). Jesus said that His coming is to be heralded with "a great sound of a trumpet" (Matt. 24:31), and Paul repeats this expression, "at the last trump" and "the trumpet shall sound" (1 Cor. 15:52). This glorious sound will assemble to Himself all the saints in glory and the saints on earth.

> Some from earth, from glory some,
> Severed only till He come.

As to the time of the Rapture, Scripture is silent. Jesus may appear at any moment. He himself hinted that His return might be after a long time and seemed to suggest that it would be wise to prepare for a delay (see Matt. 25:19). Lest saints should lose hope through His apparent tarrying, Peter reminds them that in the Lord's reckoning a thousand years are but a day (2 Pet. 3:8). What Paul calls "that blessed hope" (Titus 2:13), he links to the commemoration of the Lord's Supper. "For as often as ye eat this bread, and drink this cup, ye do show the Lord's death *till he come*" (1 Cor. 11:26, italics added). John would have believers remember that when they ultimately see Jesus, they will be like Him (see 1 John 3:1–3).

The question is: Are we like Him in character now? Does the prospect of seeing Him at any moment exercise a sanctifying influence over the phase of our present life? Is ours

> . . . A life all lily-fair,
> And fragrant as the place
> Where seraphs are?

Horatius Bonar, the Scottish saintly minister and poet who gave us some of our best hymns, firmly believed in the return of the Lord he dearly loved. Bonar preached and wrote about such a glorious event. He taught himself, however, to live constantly as one ready to hail his Lord's arrival. While retiring at night and closing the curtains, he would repeat the words, "Perhaps tonight, Lord!" In the morning when he awoke, drew aside the curtains, and looked out on another dawn, he would pray, "Perhaps today, Lord!" Can we say that this is our attitude?

> Some time, some ordinary day will come—
> A busy day like this—filled to the brim
> With ordinary tasks—perhaps so full
> That we have little thought or care for Him,
> And there will be no hint from the silent skies,

No sign, no clash of cymbals, roll of drums;
And yet that ordinary day will be
The very day in which our Lord will come.

In a few of His parables, Jesus stressed the necessity of having His return uppermost in our thoughts. The parable of the faithful and wise servants is a discourse on watchfulness in view of His coming (see Matt. 24:45–51). The parable of the ten virgins teaches the lesson of preparedness for His coming as the bridegroom (see Matt. 25:1–13). The parable of the ten talents implies that service here below is a training for a more glorified form of service above (see Matt. 25:14–30).

THE REIGN OF CHRIST

After our gathering together, which is referred to as "the day of Christ," events move swiftly in connection with the coming of the "day of the Lord." The majority of our Lord's sayings about His Second Coming, spoken during His last days before His death, are associated with the great Tribulation. It follows the disappearance of the saints from earth at the Rapture. These events will then occur: His judgment of the living nations; the inauguration of His millennial reign, when for a thousand years He will rule without a rival; and the final assize, when he will assign the Devil, all satanic forces, and the wicked dead to eternal perdition.

In this terminus of a future and final catastrophe, Jesus Himself is the Judge; no thought in His teaching is more frequent than this. Thus a marked feature in His solemn words about this concluding judgment is His phrase, "that day" (Mark 13:32)! As this judgment is to be in the presence of His angels, they will attend Him, like courtiers surround a king. They will assist Him in his role as the Vice Regent of God. The angelic host gladly welcomed the baby Jesus as He came to destroy the works of the devil. At the end, angels will magnify Him for his final triumph over Satan and his diabolical works. There is no more dreadful scene depicted in Scripture than that of the Great White Throne (see Rev. 20:7–15). Saints have no need to worry.

If we are at the first judgment, the judgment seat of Christ for believers and believers only, with its assessment of rewards and positions in future service (see Rom. 14:10; 1 Cor. 3:12–15; 2 Cor. 5:10), then, bless God, we shall not be present at the final Judgment. It will complete the condemnation already announced (see John 3:18,36). After the description of the new heaven and new earth, forming one of the most precious chapters in the Bible (see Rev. 21), we have the concluding chapter of the Bible with its final invitations, warnings, and promises. In Revelation 22, Jesus returns to the blessed hope He promised His own when He said, "I will come again" (John 14:3). Three times over Jesus says, "I come quickly" (Rev. 22:7,12,20).

Meditate on these final statements:

The last word of the Holy Spirit and the Glorified Church—"The Spirit and the bride say, Come" (Rev. 22:17).

The last word of Jesus in Scripture—"Surely I come quickly" (Rev. 22:20).

The last word of a saint—"Even so, come, Lord Jesus" (Rev. 22:20).

> Hark! what a sound, and too divine for hearing,
>   Stirs on the earth and trembles in the air!
> Is it the thunder of the Lord's appearing?
>   Is it the music of His people's prayer?
> Surely He cometh and a thousand voices
>   Shout to the saints and to the deaf and dumb!
> Surely He cometh, and the earth rejoices,
>   Glad in His coming, Who hath sworn, I *come!*